THE ULTIMATE
MEAL-PREP COOKBOOK

100 EASY RECIPES FOR LOW-CALORIE, HIGH-ENERGY LIVING

ELOISA MCCARTHY

Disclaimer

The information contained in this eBook is meant to serve as a comprehensive collection of strategies that the author of this eBook has done research about. Summaries, strategies, tips and tricks are only recommendation by the author, and reading this eBook will not guarantee that one's results will exactly mirror the author's results. The author of the eBook has made all reasonable effort to provide current and accurate information for the readers of the eBook. The author and its associates will not be held liable for any unintentional error or omissions that may be found. The material in the eBook may include information by third parties. Third party materials comprise of opinions expressed by their owners. As such, the author of the eBook does not assume responsibility or liability for any third party material or opinions. Whether because of the progression of the internet, or the unforeseen changes in company policy and editorial submission guidelines, what is stated as fact at the time of this writing may become outdated or inapplicable later.

TABLE OF CONTENTS

INTRODUCTION

Meal prep is the secret weapon of all those effortlessly fit celebrities who roam around LA—it's what many of the top private chefs do to keep their clients on track and happy.

Meal prep makes it easy to have a perfectly portioned, low-calorie, whole food meal at your fingertips any time. By meal prepping on the weekends and dividing meals into just-right, calorie-controlled portions, it's just as easy to grab your prepped Korean bibimbap bowl on a busy weeknight as it is to grab a store-bought, sodium-laden version or a take-out, high-calorie version.

BREAKFAST

1. Freezer Breakfast Burritos

Yields 12 burritos

Ingredients

- ½ cup (80g) chopped onions

- 1 cup (70g) diced mushrooms

- 2 cups (80g) chopped spinach

- 2 cups eggs (480g) taco seasoning (packet or homemade)

- 1 cup (100g) diced tomatoes

- 12-16 oz. (340-450g) cooked ground turkey/sausage

- 12 tortillas (low-carb, sprouted grain and whole wheat are all great light options)

- low fat cheese, optional

Directions

a) Sauté onions in a little cooking spray until translucent and tender, just a few minutes. Add mushrooms and spinach. Allow spinach to wilt.

b) Whisk eggs and egg whites together. Pour into heated skillet and scramble eggs until cooked.

c) Add meat, taco seasoning, and tomatoes, stirring well to combine and coat.

d) Fill tortillas with mixture and top with a pinch of low fat cheese if desired.

e) Fold tortillas into burritos, tucking in the sides so the filling is fully enclosed, and wrap in plastic wrap to maintain form. Freeze!

f) When you're ready to enjoy, reheat in microwave for about 1-2 minutes, turning halfway.

2. Overnight Oats

Yields 1 jar

Ingredients

- $\frac{1}{2}$ cup (40g) oats (any kind will do!)
- $\frac{1}{2}$ cup (120mL) almond milk (or milk of choice)
- 1 scoop chocolate protein powder (optional)
- $\frac{1}{4}$ cup (75g) mashed banana
- 2 Tablespoons Greek yogurt
- 1 Tablespoons peanut butter
- stevia, honey or sweetener of choice, to taste

Directions

a) Combine all ingredients in a jar, adjusting sweetness and texture to taste.

b) Place jar in refrigerator overnight, or for at least 4 hours.

c) Remove from refrigerator and devour cold!

d) Make up to 5 days in advance and store in the fridge.

3. Vegetarian Breakfast Bake

Yields 12 servings

Ingredients

- 1 cup (160g) onion, chopped

- 1 Tablespoons minced garlic

- 4 oz. (115g) sliced mushrooms

- 1 package frozen spinach, or 1 bag fresh (254g)

- 1 10 oz. (280g) bag frozen broccoli, thawed

- 4 slices (112g) whole wheat or sprouted grain bread, cut into cubes (about $\frac{1}{2}$")

- 4 eggs

- 3 cups (720g) egg whites/substitute

- 2 cups (480mL) almond milk

- $\frac{1}{2}$ cup (60g) Swiss cheese

- $\frac{1}{2}$ teaspoons nutmeg

- $\frac{3}{4}$ teaspoons salt (to taste)

- $\frac{1}{2}$ teaspoons pepper (to taste)

- $\frac{1}{2}$ cup (60g) low fat cheddar cheese

Directions

a) Sauté onion, garlic, mushrooms and spinach in a skillet using cooking spray (you can use oil but nutritional data will differ). Combine with thawed broccoli. Set aside.

b) Spread bread cubes over bottom of baking dish.

c) Whisk together eggs, egg whites/substitute, almond milk, Swiss cheese, nutmeg, salt and pepper.

d) Layer vegetables over bread, maintaining 2 layers to the best of your ability.

e) Pour egg mixture over entire baking dish, completely covering both layers of bread/vegetables.

f) Cover and refrigerate overnight (about 8 hours).

g) In the morning, preheat oven to 350F (180C). Top the bake with cheddar cheese. Bake 50-60 minutes, until cheese begins to brown and eggs are cooked through.

h) Devour warm, save to reheat, or enjoy cold later on!

i) Lasts 5 days in the fridge, or 3-4 months in the freezer.

4. Freezer Breakfast Sandwiches

Yields 6 sandwiches

Ingredients

- 1 ½ cups eggs (360g) or egg whites/substitute, seasoned with salt and pepper

- 6 English muffins (whole wheat or sprouted grain)

- 12 slices deli chicken or ham

- 6 slices thinly sliced cheddar cheese

Directions

a) Preheat oven to 375F (190C).

b) Spray down 6 small ramekins with cooking spray and pour ¼ cup (60g) egg mixture into each. Bake for 15-20 minutes, until completely set. Set aside and allow to cool.

c) Once cool to the touch, assemble sandwiches. Place egg on bottom of English muffin, followed by 2 slices of deli meat, 1 slice of thin cheddar cheese, and the top of the muffin.

d) Wrap in plastic wrap and transfer to a larger plastic storage bag or plastic storage container.

5. Banana Nut Mini-Muffins

Yields 24 mini muffins

Ingredients

- 2 bananas, mashed

- 1 egg

- ¾ cup (60g) oat flour

- 2 Tablespoons peanut butter

- 1 teaspoons vanilla

- ¾ teaspoons baking powder

- ½ teaspoons cinnamon

- 1-2 Tablespoons stevia or granulated sweetener of choice, to taste

- ¼ cup (30g) crushed walnuts, plus additional for topping if desired

Directions

a) Preheat oven to 375F (190C).

b) Mix all ingredients together, combining well. Adjust sweetness to taste- the bananas are a great natural sweetener so you may not need much!

c) Transfer to mini muffin tin that has been sprayed with cooking spray, filling about $\frac{3}{4}$ of the way full.

d) Bake 10-12 minutes, until a toothpick comes out clean and they are a light golden brown.

e) Allow to cool slightly before removing from pan and devouring!

f) Lasts 1 week in the fridge, or 2-3 months in the freezer.

6. Turkey Meatloaf Muffins

Yields 24 mini meatloaf muffins

Ingredients

- 20 oz. (600g) extra lean ground turkey breast
- ½ cup (120g) egg whites
- ½ cup (40g) oats
- 1 teaspoon yellow mustard
- 1 teaspoons Dijon mustard
- 1 cup (40g) chopped spinach
- ½ cup (80g) onion
- ¼ cup (45g) red bell pepper
- ¼ cup (25g) celery
- 1 teaspoons minced garlic
- ½ teaspoons garlic powder salt and pepper to taste

Directions

a) Preheat oven to 350F (180C).

b) Mix all ingredients in a bowl.

c) Divide meat mixture into mini muffin tin sprayed with cooking spray - a 1-Tablespoons cookie scooper works well to distribute.

d) Bake for about 15-20 minutes.

e) Lasts 5 days in the fridge, or 3-4 months in the freezer.

7. Bean Salsa Salad

Yields about 8 cups

Ingredients

- 1 15 oz. can (425g) black beans, drained/rinsed
- 1 15 oz. can (425g) garbanzo beans or white beans, drained/rinsed
- 1 15 oz. can (425g) yellow corn, drained/rinsed
- 1 10 oz. can (280g) diced tomatoes and chiles
- 1 Tablespoons minced garlic
- ½ cup (115g) chopped green onion
- 2 Tablespoons cilantro
- ½ cup (240mL) mojo marinade

Directions

a) Mix all ingredients together in a bowl.

b) Allow to chill in the refrigerator for a few hours.

c) Lasts up to a week in the fridge.

8. Veggie-Packed Frittata

Yields 1 serving

Ingredients

- 1-2 cups (180-360g) diced vegetables

- $\frac{1}{2}$ cup (20g) spinach, chopped

- $\frac{3}{4}$ cup (180g) egg whites seasoned with salt and pepper

- Salsa for topping

Directions

a) Pre-heat oven to broil.

b) Heat a large skillet over medium-high heat. Spray with nonstick cooking spray.

c) Add vegetables and spinach. Sauté in skillet for 3-5 minutes until veggies are tender and spinach is wilted.

d) Pour egg mixture into skillet. Allow bottom to set (3-4 minutes). Use your spatula to go around the perimeter of the frittata, and lift the set egg.

e) place the skillet in the broiler for 3 minutes.

f) Carefully remove and plate. Cut and serve with salsa!

9. All-American breakfast

Ingredients

- 12 ounces' russet potatoes, diced

- 3 tablespoons olive oil, divided

- 2 cloves garlic, minced

- $\frac{1}{2}$ teaspoon dried thyme

- Kosher salt and freshly ground black pepper, to taste

- 8 large eggs, lightly beaten

- $\frac{1}{4}$ cup shredded reduced-fat Mexican cheese blend

- 4 slices bacon

- 12 ounces' broccoli florets (2 to 3 cups)

Directions

a) Preheat the oven to 400 degrees F. Lightly oil a baking sheet or coat with nonstick spray.

b) On the prepared baking sheet, toss the potatoes with 1 tablespoon of the olive oil, the garlic, and thyme; season with salt and pepper. Arrange in a single layer. Bake for 25 to 30 minutes, until golden brown and crisp; set aside.

c) Heat the remaining 2 tablespoons olive oil in a large skillet over medium-high heat. Add the eggs and whisk until they just begin to set. Season with salt and pepper and continue cooking until thickened and no visible liquid egg remains, 3 to 5 minutes. Top with the cheese, transfer to a bowl, and set aside.

d) Add the bacon to the skillet and cook until brown and crispy, 6 to 8 minutes. Transfer to a paper towel-lined plate.

e) Meanwhile, place the broccoli florets in a steamer or colander set over about an inch of boiling water in a pan. Cover and steam for 5 minutes, or until crisp-tender and vibrant green.

f) Divide the potatoes, eggs, bacon, and broccoli into meal prep containers. Will keep covered in the refrigerator 3 to 4 days. Reheat in the microwave in 30-second intervals until heated through.

10. Breakfast stuffed sweet potatoes

Ingredients

- 2 medium sweet potatoes
- 1 tablespoon olive oil
- 2 tablespoons diced red bell pepper
- 1 garlic clove, minced
- $\frac{1}{2}$ teaspoon crushed red pepper flakes
- 4 cups baby spinach
- 4 large eggs, lightly beaten
- 1 teaspoon Italian seasoning
- Kosher salt and freshly ground black pepper, to taste
- $\frac{1}{2}$ cup shredded reduced-fat cheddar cheese
- 1 tablespoon chopped fresh chives (optional)

Directions

a) Preheat the oven to 400 degrees F. Place the potatoes on a baking sheet and bake for 45 minutes to 1 hour, until they are tender and easily pierced with a fork. Let sit until cool enough to handle. Don't turn off the oven.

b) Cut each potato in half horizontally, then carefully scoop out the center of each half, leaving about $\frac{1}{2}$ inch of potato on the skin. Reserve the flesh for another use.

c) Heat the olive oil in a large skillet over medium-high heat. Add the bell pepper and cook, stirring frequently, until tender, 3 to 4 minutes. Stir in the garlic and red pepper flakes, and then the spinach and stir until wilted, 2 to 3 minutes. Add the eggs and Italian seasoning; cook, stirring occasionally with a spatula, until just set, 2 to 3 minutes; season with salt and pepper to taste.

d) Add the egg mixture to the potato skins and sprinkle with the cheese. Place back on the baking sheet and bake in the 400-degree oven for 5 minutes, or until the cheese has melted.

e) Portion into meal prep containers. Will keep covered in the refrigerator 3 to 4 days. Reheat in the microwave in 30-

second intervals until heated through. Garnish with chives, if desired, and serve.

11.   Blueberry oatmeal yogurt pancakes

Ingredients

- ½ plus ⅓ cup white whole wheat flour

- ½ cup old-fashioned rolled oats

- 1 ½ teaspoons sugar

- ½ teaspoon baking powder

- ½ teaspoon baking soda

- ¼ teaspoon kosher salt

- ¾ cup Greek yogurt

- ½ cup 2% milk

- 1 teaspoon olive oil

- 1 large egg

- ½ cup blueberries

- 12 strawberries, thinly sliced

- 2 kiwis, peeled and thinly sliced

- ¼ cup maple syrup

Directions

a) Preheat a nonstick griddle to 350 degrees F or heat a nonstick skillet over medium-high heat. Lightly coat the griddle or skillet with nonstick spray.

b) In a large bowl, combine the flour, oats, sugar, baking powder, baking soda, and salt. In a large glass measuring cup or another bowl, whisk together the yogurt, milk, olive oil, and egg. Pour the wet mixture over the dry Ingredients and stir with a rubber spatula just until moist. Add the blueberries and gently toss to combine.

c) Working in batches, scoop ⅓ cup batter for each pancake onto the griddle and cook until bubbles appear on top and the underside is nicely browned, about 2 minutes. Flip and cook the pancakes on the other side, 1 to 2 minutes longer.

d) Divide the pancakes, strawberries, kiwis, and maple syrup into meal prep containers. Will keep covered in the refrigerator 3 to 4 days. To reheat, place in the microwave in 30-second intervals until heated through.

12. Buddha breakfast bowls

Ingredients

- 2 cups low-sodium vegetable stock
- 1 cup brown rice
- $\frac{1}{4}$ cup freshly grated Parmesan
- 1 teaspoon dried thyme
- Kosher salt and freshly ground black pepper, to taste
- 1 cup Brussels sprouts
- 1 cup cherry tomatoes
- 8 ounces cremini mushrooms
- 2 tablespoons olive oil
- 3 cloves garlic, minced
- 1 teaspoon Italian seasoning
- 4 large eggs
- 2 tablespoons chopped fresh chives (optional)

Directions

a) In a large saucepan of vegetable stock, cook the rice according to package instructions. Stir in the Parmesan and thyme and season with salt and pepper to taste.

b) Preheat the oven to 400 degrees F. Lightly oil a baking sheet or coat with nonstick spray.

c) On the prepared baking sheet, combine the Brussels sprouts, tomatoes, and mushrooms with the olive oil, garlic, and Italian seasoning; season with salt and pepper. Gently toss to combine and arrange in a single layer. Bake for 13 to 14 minutes, until the sprouts are tender.

d) Meanwhile, place the eggs in a small saucepan and cover with cold water by 1 inch. Bring to a boil and cook for 1 minute. Cover the pan with a tight-fitting lid and remove from the heat; let sit for 5 to 6 minutes. Rinse the eggs under cold water for 30 seconds to stop the cooking. Peel and cut in half.

e) Divide the rice into meal prep containers. Top with the Brussels sprouts, tomatoes, mushrooms, and eggs, and garnish with chives, if desired. Will keep covered in the refrigerator 2 to 3 days. Reheat in the microwave in 30-second intervals until heated through.

13.   Mason jar chia puddings

Ingredients

- 1 ¼ cups 2% milk
- 1 cup 2% plain Greek yogurt
- ½ cup chia seeds
- 2 tablespoons honey
- 2 tablespoons sugar
- 1 tablespoon orange zest
- 2 teaspoons vanilla extract
- ¾ cup segmented oranges
- ¾ cup segmented tangerines
- ½ cup segmented grapefruit

Directions

a) In a large bowl, whisk together the milk, Greek yogurt, chia seeds, honey, sugar, orange zest, vanilla, and salt until well combined.

b) Divide mixture evenly into four (16-ounce) mason jars. Refrigerate overnight, or up to 5 days.

c) Serve cold, topped with oranges, tangerines, and grapefruit.

14.   Rainbow Lime Chia Pudding

Ingredients

- 1 ¼ cups 2% milk
- 1 cup 2% plain Greek yogurt
- ½ cup chia seeds
- 2 tablespoons honey
- 2 tablespoons sugar
- 2 teaspoons lime zest
- 2 tablespoons freshly squeezed lime juice
- 1 teaspoon vanilla extract
- 1 cup chopped strawberries and blueberries
- ½ cup diced mango and ½ cup diced kiwi

Directions

a) In a large bowl, whisk together the milk, yogurt, chia seeds, honey, sugar, lime zest, lime juice, vanilla, and salt until well combined.

b) Divide the mixture evenly into four (16-ounce) mason jars. Cover and refrigerate overnight, or up to 5 days.

c) Serve cold, topped with strawberries, mango, kiwi, and blueberries.

15.   Tropical Coconut Chia Pudding

Ingredients

- 1 (13.5-ounce) can coconut milk

- 1 cup 2% plain Greek yogurt

- $\frac{1}{2}$ cup chia seeds

- 2 tablespoons honey

- 2 tablespoons sugar

- 1 teaspoon vanilla extract

- Pinch of kosher salt

- 1 cup diced mango

- 1 cup diced pineapple

- 2 tablespoons shredded coconut

Directions

a) In a large bowl, whisk together the coconut milk, yogurt, chia seeds, honey, sugar, vanilla, and salt until well combined.

b) Divide the mixture evenly into four (16-ounce) mason jars. Cover and refrigerate overnight, or up to 5 days.

c) Serve cold, topped with mango and pineapple and sprinkled with coconut.

16.   Blueberry lemon cheesecake oats

Ingredients

- ¼ cup non-fat Greek yogurt

- 2 tablespoons blueberry yogurt

- ¼ cup blueberries

- 1 teaspoon grated lemon zest

- 1 teaspoon honey

Directions

a) Combine the oats and milk in a 16-ounce mason jar; top with desired toppings.

b) Refrigerate overnight or up to 3 days; serve cold.

17.   Breakfast croissant sandwiches

Ingredients

- 1 tablespoon olive oil

- 4 large eggs, lightly beaten

- Kosher salt and freshly ground black pepper, to taste

- 8 mini croissants, halved horizontally

- 4 ounces thinly sliced ham

- 4 slices cheddar cheese, halved

Directions

a) Heat the olive oil in a large skillet over medium-high heat. Add the eggs and cook, stirring gently with a silicone or heat-proof spatula, until they just begin to set; season with salt and pepper. Continue cooking until thickened and no visible liquid egg remains, 3 to 5 minutes.

b) Fill the croissants with the eggs, ham, and cheese to make 8 sandwiches. Wrap tightly in plastic wrap and freeze for up to 1 month.

c) To reheat, remove the plastic wrap from a frozen sandwich and wrap in a paper towel. Microwave, flipping halfway, for 1 to 2 minutes, until heated through completely.

18.   Garlic mushroom oatmeal

Ingredients

- 2 cups old-fashioned rolled oats
- Kosher salt and freshly ground black pepper, to taste
- 1 tablespoon olive oil
- 4 cloves garlic, minced
- $\frac{1}{4}$ cup diced shallots
- 8 ounces cremini mushrooms, thinly sliced
- $\frac{1}{2}$ cup frozen peas
- 1 teaspoon dried thyme
- $\frac{1}{2}$ teaspoon dried rosemary
- 2 cups baby spinach
- Grated zest of 1 lemon
- $\frac{1}{4}$ cup freshly grated Parmesan (optional)

Directions

a) Combine the oats, 3 $\frac{1}{2}$ cups water, and a pinch of salt in a small saucepan over medium heat. Cook, stirring occasionally, until the oats have softened, about 5 minutes.

b) Heat the olive oil in a large skillet over medium-high heat. Add the garlic and shallots and cook, stirring frequently, until fragrant, about 2 minutes. Add the mushrooms, peas, thyme, and rosemary and cook, stirring occasionally, until tender and browned, 5 to 6 minutes; season with salt and pepper. Stir in the spinach until wilted, about 2 minutes.

c) Stir the oats and lemon zest into the vegetables until well combined. Divide the mixture into meal prep containers and garnish with Parmesan, if desired. Refrigerate for up to 3 days.

d) To serve, stir in up to $\frac{1}{4}$ cup water, 1 tablespoon at a time, until desired consistency is reached. The oatmeal can then be reheated in the microwave in 30-second intervals until heated through.

19.   PB-Oatmeal breakfast bowl

Ingredients

- ½ cup old-fashioned rolled oats

- Pinch of kosher salt

- 2 tablespoons raspberries

- 2 tablespoons blueberries

- 1 tablespoon chopped almonds

- ½ teaspoon chia seeds

- 1 banana, thinly sliced

- 2 teaspoons peanut butter, warmed

Directions

a) Combine 1 cup water, the oats, and salt in a small saucepan. Cook over medium heat, stirring occasionally, until the oats have softened, about 5 minutes.

b) Add the oatmeal to a meal prep container. Top with the raspberries, blueberries, almonds, chia seeds, and banana, and drizzle with the warm peanut butter. Keeps covered in the refrigerator for 3 to 4 days.

c) The oatmeal can be served cold or reheated. Reheat in the microwave at 30-second intervals until heated through.

20.   Protein power waffles

Ingredients

- 6 large eggs
- 2 cups cottage cheese
- 2 cups old-fashioned rolled oats
- $\frac{1}{2}$ teaspoon vanilla extract
- Pinch of kosher salt
- 3 cups non-fat plain yogurt
- 1 $\frac{1}{2}$ cups raspberries
- 1 $\frac{1}{2}$ cups blueberries

Directions

a) Preheat a waffle iron to medium high. Lightly oil the top and bottom of the iron or coat with nonstick spray.

b) Combine the eggs, cottage cheese, oats, vanilla, and salt in a blender and blend until smooth.

c) Pour a scant $\frac{1}{2}$ cup of the egg mixture into the waffle iron, close gently, and cook until golden brown and crisp, 4 to 5 minutes.

d) Place the waffles, yogurt, raspberries, and blueberries into meal prep containers.

21.   Smoked salmon mini-bagel bar

Ingredients

- ¼ cup ⅓-less-fat cream cheese, at room temperature
- 1 green onion, thinly sliced
- 1 tablespoon chopped fresh dill
- 1 teaspoon grated lemon zest
- ¼ teaspoon garlic powder
- 4 whole wheat mini bagels
- 8 ounces smoked salmon
- ½ cup thinly sliced English cucumber
- ½ cup thinly sliced red onion
- 2 plum tomatoes, thinly sliced
- 4 teaspoons capers, drained and rinsed

Directions

a) In a small bowl, combine the cream cheese, green onion, dill, lemon zest, and garlic powder.

b) Place the cheese mixture, bagels, salmon, cucumber, onion, tomatoes, and capers into meal prep containers and add lemon wedges, if desired. These keep in the refrigerator for up to 2 days.

SMOOTHIES

22.   Berry beet smoothie

Ingredients

TO PREP

- 1 (9 ounce) package cooked beets
- 1 cup frozen strawberries
- 1 cup frozen raspberries
- 1 tablespoon chia seeds

TO SERVE

- 1 cup unsweetened vanilla almond milk
- $\frac{1}{2}$ cup 2% Greek yogurt
- 2 tablespoons honey
- 1 teaspoon vanilla extract

Directions

a) Combine the beets, strawberries, raspberries, and chia seeds in a large bowl. Divide among 4 ziplock freezer bags. Freeze for up to a month, until ready to serve.

b) Place the contents of one bag in a blender and add $\frac{1}{4}$ cup almond milk, 2 tablespoons yogurt, 1 $\frac{1}{2}$ teaspoons honey, and $\frac{1}{4}$ teaspoon vanilla. Blend until smooth. Serve immediately.

23. Banana-peanut butter "milkshake"

Ingredients

TO PREP

- 3 medium bananas, sliced
- ⅓ cup peanut butter powder (such as PB2)
- ⅓ cup vanilla protein powder
- 3 pitted dates
- ¼ teaspoon ground cinnamon

TO SERVE

- 1 cup unsweetened almond milk
- ½ cup Greek yogurt
- Cinnamon (optional)

Directions

a) Combine the bananas, PB powder, protein powder, dates, and cinnamon in a large bowl. Divide among 5 ziplock freezer bags and freeze for up to a month, until ready to serve

b) Place the contents of one bag in a blender and add a generous 3 tablespoons almond milk, 1 ½ tablespoons yogurt, and ¼ cup ice. Blend until smooth. Sprinkle with cinnamon, if using, and serve immediately.

24. Antioxidant acai berry smoothie

Ingredients

TO PREP

- 2 (3.88-ounce) packages frozen acai puree, thawed

- 1 cup frozen raspberries

- 1 cup frozen blueberries

- 1 cup frozen blackberries

- 1 cup frozen strawberries

- $\frac{1}{2}$ cup pomegranate seeds

TO SERVE

- $1\frac{1}{2}$ cup pomegranate juice

Directions

a) Combine the acai, raspberries, blueberries, blackberries, strawberries, and pomegranate seeds in a large bowl. Divide the mixture among 4 ziplock freezer bags. Freeze for up to a month, until ready to serve.

b) Place the contents of one bag in a blender, add a generous ⅓ cup pomegranate juice, and blend until smooth. Serve immediately.

25. Berry melon smoothie

Ingredients

TO PREP

- 4 cups diced frozen watermelon
- 2 cups diced cantaloupe
- 1 cup frozen raspberries
- ⅓ cup packed fresh mint leaves

TO SERVE

- 1 cup coconut water
- 4 tablespoons fresh lime juice
- 2 tablespoons honey

Directions

a) Combine the watermelon, cantaloupe, raspberries, and mint in a large bowl. Divide among 4 ziplock freezer bags and freeze for up to a month, until ready to serve.

b) TO MAKE ONE SERVING: Place the contents of one bag in a blender and add ¼ cup coconut water, 1 tablespoon lime juice, and 1 ½ teaspoons honey. Blend until smooth. Serve immediately.

26. Black forest smoothie

Ingredients

TO PREP

- 1 (16-ounce) bag frozen pitted sweet cherries
- 2 cups baby spinach
- 2 tablespoons cocoa powder
- 1 tablespoon chia seeds

TO SERVE

- 1 cup unsweetened chocolate almond milk
- $\frac{3}{4}$ cup vanilla 2% Greek yogurt
- 3 teaspoons maple syrup
- 1 teaspoon vanilla extract

Directions

a) Combine the cherries, spinach, cocoa powder, and chia seeds in a large bowl. Divide among 4 ziplock freezer bags. Freeze for up to a month, until ready to serve.

b) TO MAKE ONE SERVING: Place the contents of one bag in a blender and add $\frac{1}{4}$ cup almond milk, 3 tablespoons yogurt, $\frac{3}{4}$ teaspoon maple syrup, and $\frac{1}{4}$ teaspoon vanilla. Blend until smooth. Serve immediately.

27.   Blueberry pie smoothie

Ingredients

TO PREP

- 2 ½ cups frozen blueberries

- 1 banana, sliced

- 2 whole cinnamon graham crackers, broken into pieces

- 1 tablespoon almond butter

TO SERVE

- 1 cup unsweetened vanilla almond milk

- ½ cup 2% Greek yogurt

- 3 teaspoons honey

Directions

a) Combine the blueberries, banana, graham crackers, and almond butter in a large bowl. Divide among 4 ziplock freezer bags. Freeze for up to a month, until ready to serve.

b) TO MAKE ONE SERVING: Place the contents of one bag in a blender and add ¼ cup almond milk, 2 tablespoons yogurt, and ¾ teaspoon honey. Blend until smooth. Serve immediately.

28. Carrot ginger smoothie

Ingredients

TO PREP

- 2 navel oranges, peeled, chopped, and seeds removed

- 2 cups frozen sliced carrots

- 1 ½ cups diced frozen pineapple

- 1 tablespoon finely chopped peeled fresh ginger

TO SERVE

- 1 cup carrot juice

- 1 cup vanilla Greek yogurt

- 3 teaspoons honey

Directions

a) Combine the oranges, carrots, pineapple, and ginger in a large bowl. Divide among 4 ziplock freezer bags. Freeze for up to a month, until ready to serve.

b) TO MAKE ONE SERVING: Place the contents of one bag in a blender and add ¼ cup carrot juice, ¼ cup yogurt, and ¾ teaspoon honey. Blend until smooth. Serve immediately.

29. Creamy green goddess smoothie

Ingredients

TO PREP

- 1 avocado, halved, pitted, and peeled

- 2 cups baby spinach

- 2 cups baby kale

- 1 $\frac{1}{2}$ cups diced pineapple

- 1 cup chopped sugar snap peas

- $\frac{1}{3}$ cup vanilla protein powder

TO SERVE

- 1 $\frac{1}{2}$ cups unsweetened almond milk

Directions

a) Combine the avocado, spinach, kale, pineapple, snap peas, and protein powder in a large bowl. Divide among 6 ziplock freezer bags. Freeze for up to a month, until ready to serve.

b) TO MAKE ONE SERVING: Place the contents of one bag in a blender and add $\frac{1}{4}$ cup almond milk. Blend until smooth. Serve immediately.

30.   Garden kiwi smoothie

Ingredients

TO PREP

- 4 kiwis, peeled and sliced
- 2 cups packed baby spinach
- 1 cup sliced banana
- 2 tablespoons chia seeds

TO SERVE

- 1 cup vanilla Greek yogurt
- 1 head Boston lettuce
- 3 Persian cucumbers, sliced

Directions

a) Combine the kiwi, spinach, banana, and chia seeds in a large bowl. Divide among 4 ziplock freezer bags. Freeze for up to a month, until ready to serve.

b) TO MAKE ONE SERVING: Place the contents of one bag in a blender and add $\frac{1}{4}$ cup yogurt, $\frac{1}{2}$ cup torn lettuce leaves, and sliced cucumber. Blend until smooth. Serve immediately.

31. Green detox smoothie

Ingredients

TO PREP

- 2 cups baby spinach

- 2 cups baby kale

- 2 stalks celery, chopped

- 1 medium green apple, cored and chopped

- 1 cup sliced banana

- 1 tablespoon grated fresh ginger

- 1 tablespoon chia seeds

TO SERVE

- 1 cup unsweetened almond milk

- 3 teaspoons honey

Directions

a) Combine the spinach, kale, celery, apple, banana, ginger, and chia seeds in a large bowl. Divide among 4 ziplock freezer bags. Freeze for up to a month, until ready to serve.

b) TO MAKE ONE SERVING: Place the contents of one bag in a blender and add $\frac{1}{4}$ cup almond milk and $\frac{3}{4}$ teaspoon honey. Blend until smooth. Serve immediately.

32.　　Green protein smoothie

Ingredients

TO PREP

- 3 cups baby spinach
- 1 banana, sliced
- $\frac{1}{2}$ avocado, pitted and peeled
- $\frac{1}{2}$ cup blueberries
- 2 handfuls fresh parsley leaves
- 8 tablespoons vanilla protein powder

TO SERVE

- 1 cup sliced cucumber
- $\frac{3}{4}$ cup unsweetened almond milk

Directions

a) Combine the spinach, banana, avocado, blueberries, parsley, and protein powder in a large bowl. Divide among 4 ziplock freezer bags. Freeze for up to a month, until ready to serve.

b) TO MAKE ONE SERVING: Place the contents of one bag in a blender and add $\frac{1}{4}$ cup cucumber and 3 tablespoons almond milk. Blend until smooth. Serve immediately.

33.   Carrot turmeric smoothie

Ingredients

TO PREP

- 1 cup sliced frozen carrots

- 1 banana, sliced

- 1 medium green apple, cored and chopped

- 1 (1-inch) piece fresh ginger, peeled and sliced

- 1 teaspoon ground turmeric, or more to taste

TO SERVE

- 1 cup carrot juice

- $\frac{1}{2}$ cup 2% Greek yogurt

- 4 teaspoons maple syrup

- $\frac{1}{2}$ teaspoon vanilla extract

Directions

a) Combine the carrots, banana, apple, ginger, and turmeric in a large bowl. Divide among 4 ziplock freezer bags.

b) Place the contents of one bag in a blender and add $\frac{1}{4}$ cup carrot juice, 2 tablespoons yogurt, a generous teaspoon maple syrup, $\frac{1}{8}$ teaspoon vanilla, and $\frac{1}{4}$ cup ice. Blend until smooth. Serve immediately.

34.   Peach melba smoothie

Ingredients

TO PREP

- 1 (16-ounce) package frozen sliced peaches

- 1 cup frozen raspberries

- 1 orange, peeled and seeded

- ⅓ cup vanilla protein powder

TO SERVE

- ½ cup orange juice

- 2 tablespoons fresh lime juice

- 3 teaspoons honey

- 1 ½ teaspoons vanilla extract

Directions

a) Combine the peaches, raspberries, orange, and protein powder in a large bowl. Divide among 6 ziplock freezer bags. Freeze for up to a month, until ready to serve.

b) Place the contents of one bag in a blender and add 4 teaspoons orange juice, 1 teaspoon lime juice, ½ teaspoon honey, and a generous ¼ teaspoon vanilla. Blend until smooth. Serve immediately.

35.   Rainbow coconut smoothie

Ingredients

TO PREP

- 2 tangerines, peeled and segmented
- 1 cup diced pineapple
- 1 cup diced mango
- 1 cup sliced strawberries
- 1 cup blueberries
- 1 cup blackberries
- 1 kiwi, peeled and sliced
- 2 cups baby spinach
- $\frac{1}{2}$ cup flaked coconut

TO SERVE

- 2 cups coconut water

Directions

a) Combine the tangerines, pineapple, mango, strawberries, blueberries, blackberries, kiwi, spinach, and coconut in a large bowl. Divide among 6 ziplock freezer bags. Freeze for up to a month, until ready to serve.

b) TO MAKE ONE SERVING: Place the contents of one bag in a blender and add ⅓ cup coconut water. Blend until smooth. Serve immediately.

36.   Tropical green smoothie

Ingredients

TO PREP

- 4 cups baby spinach

- 1 cup frozen mango

- $\frac{3}{4}$ cup frozen pineapple

- 1 banana, sliced

- 2 tangerines, peeled and segmented

- 4 teaspoons chia seeds

TO SERVE

- 3 cups coconut water

Directions

a) Combine the spinach, mango, pineapple, banana, tangerines, and chia seeds in a large bowl. Divide among 4 ziplock freezer bags. Freeze for up to a month, until ready to serve.

b) TO MAKE ONE SERVING: Place the contents of one bag in a blender and add $\frac{3}{4}$ cup coconut water. Blend until smooth. Serve immediately.

37.   Tropical Quinoa Smoothie

Yields 1 smoothie

Ingredients

- $\frac{1}{4}$ cup (45g) cooked quinoa

- $\frac{1}{4}$ cup (60mL) light coconut milk (or milk of choice)

- $\frac{1}{3}$ cup (50g) frozen mango chunks $\frac{1}{3}$ cup (45g) frozen pineapple chunks $\frac{1}{2}$ frozen banana

- 1 Tablespoons unsweetened shredded coconut

- 1 Tablespoons coconut sugar, to taste $\frac{1}{2}$ teaspoons vanilla

Directions

a) Combine all ingredients in a blender until smooth. Adjust consistency to taste by adding more milk for a thinner smoothie, and ice or a bit of yogurt for a thicker smoothie.

b) Enjoy!

SNACK BOX

38.   Antipasto snack box for two

Ingredients

- 2 ounces thinly sliced prosciutto

- 2 ounces' salami, cubed

- 1-ounce gouda cheese, thinly sliced

- 1-ounce Parmesan cheese, thinly sliced

- $\frac{1}{4}$ cup almonds

- 2 tablespoons green olives

- 2 tablespoons black olives

Directions

a) Place prosciutto, salami, cheeses, almonds, and olives in a meal prep container.

b) Cover and refrigerate for up to 4 days.

39.   Buffalo-chicken celery snack box

Ingredients

- 1 cup leftover shredded rotisserie chicken
- 2 tablespoons Greek yogurt
- 2 tablespoons hot sauce
- $\frac{1}{4}$ teaspoon garlic powder
- $\frac{1}{4}$ teaspoon onion powder
- Kosher salt and freshly ground black pepper, to taste
- 6 stalks celery, cut in half
- $\frac{1}{2}$ cup strawberries, sliced
- $\frac{1}{2}$ cup grapes
- 2 tablespoons crumbled blue cheese
- 1 tablespoon chopped fresh parsley leaves

Directions

a) Combine the chicken, yogurt, hot sauce, garlic powder, and onion powder in a large bowl; season with salt and pepper to taste. Cover and refrigerate for up to 3 days.

b) Divide the celery sticks, strawberries, and grapes into meal prep containers.

40.   Chicken and hummus bistro box

Ingredients

- 1 pound boneless, skinless chicken breasts, cut into strips

- $\frac{1}{2}$ teaspoon garlic powder

- $\frac{1}{4}$ teaspoon onion powder

- Kosher salt and freshly ground black pepper, to taste

- 1 cucumber, thinly sliced

- 4 mini whole wheat pitas

- 1 cup cherry tomatoes

- $\frac{1}{2}$ cup hummus (homemade or store-bought)

Directions

a) Preheat a grill to medium-high heat. Season the chicken with the garlic powder, onion powder, salt, and pepper.

b) Add the chicken to the grill and cook, flipping once, until cooked through and the juices run clear, 5 to 6 minutes on each side; set aside until cool.

c) Divide the chicken, cucumber, pita bread, tomatoes, and hummus into meal prep containers. Refrigerate for up to 3 days.

41.   Chocolate-strawberry energy bites

Ingredients

- 1 cup old-fashioned rolled oats
- ½ cup unsweetened shredded coconut
- ⅓ cup cashew butter
- ¼ cup honey
- 3 tablespoons chia seeds
- ½ teaspoon vanilla extract
- ¼ teaspoon kosher salt
- ¾ cup finely chopped freeze-dried strawberries
- ¼ cup mini chocolate chips

Directions

a) Line a baking sheet with waxed paper or parchment paper; set aside.

b) In a food processor, pulse the oats and coconut until the mixture resembles a coarse flour, 5 to 6 pulses; transfer to a medium bowl.

c) Using a wooden spoon, stir in the cashew butter, honey, chia seeds, vanilla, and salt until well combined. Stir in the strawberries and chocolate chips until incorporated.

d) Knead the mixture together and form into 15 (1-inch) balls, about $1\frac{1}{2}$ tablespoons each. Place on the prepared baking sheet in a single layer.

e) Refrigerate until firm, about 1 hour. Store in an airtight container in the refrigerator for up to 1 week, or the freezer for up to 1 month.

42. Deli snack box

Ingredients

- 1 large egg

- 1 $\frac{1}{2}$ ounces thinly sliced turkey breast

- $\frac{1}{4}$ cup cherry tomatoes

- 1-ounce sharp cheddar cheese, cubed

- 4 pita bites crackers

- 1 tablespoon raw almonds

Directions

a) Place the egg in a saucepan and cover with cold water by 1 inch. Bring to a boil and cook for 1 minute. Cover the pan with a tight-fitting lid and remove from heat; let sit for 8 to 10 minutes. Drain well and let cool before peeling.

b) Place the turkey, egg, tomatoes, cheese, crackers, and almonds into a meal prep container. This can be kept in the refrigerator for up to 3 days.

43.　　　Pizza snackables

Ingredients

- 4 pita bites crackers
- 2 tablespoons shredded reduced-fat mozzarella cheese
- 2 tablespoons pizza sauce
- 2 tablespoons almonds
- 1 tablespoon mini pepperoni
- $\frac{1}{4}$ cup grapes

Directions

a) Place the crackers, cheese, pizza sauce, almonds, pepperoni, and grapes into a meal prep container.

b) Refrigerate for up to 3 days.

44. Greek chickpea power salad

Ingredients

Oregano-garlic vinaigrette

- $\frac{1}{4}$ cup extra-virgin olive oil
- 3 tablespoons red wine vinegar
- 2 teaspoons dried oregano
- 1 $\frac{1}{2}$ teaspoons whole grain mustard
- 1 clove garlic, pressed
- $\frac{1}{4}$ teaspoon sugar (optional)
- Kosher salt and freshly ground black pepper, to taste

Salad

- 1 (15-ounce) can garbanzo beans, rinsed and drained
- 1 pint grape tomatoes, halved
- 1 yellow bell pepper, diced
- 1 orange bell pepper, diced
- 2 Persian cucumbers, halved lengthwise and thinly sliced
- 1 cup chopped fresh parsley leaves
- ⅓ cup diced red onion

- 1 (4-ounce) container feta cheese, crumbled

Directions

a) FOR THE VINAIGRETTE: In a small bowl, whisk together the olive oil, vinegar, oregano, mustard, garlic, and sugar; season with salt and pepper to taste. Keeps covered in the refrigerator for 3 to 4 days.

b) Combine the garbanzo beans, tomatoes, bell peppers, cucumbers, parsley, onion, and cheese in a large bowl. Divide into meal prep containers. Will keep covered in the refrigerator 3 to 4 days.

c) To serve, pour vinaigrette on the salad and gently toss to combine.

45.   Kale chips snack box

Ingredients

Kale chips

- 1 bunch kale, stems and thick ribs removed

- 2 tablespoons olive oil

- 1 clove garlic, pressed

- Kosher salt and freshly ground black pepper, to taste

Crispy garbanzo beans

- 1 (16-ounce) can garbanzo beans, drained and rinsed

- 1 ½ tablespoons olive oil

- 1 ½ teaspoons chili lime seasoning

- 1 cup strawberries, sliced

- 1 cup grapes

- 4 tangerines, peeled and segmented

Directions

a) Preheat the oven to 375 degrees F. Lightly oil a baking sheet or coat with nonstick spray.

b) FOR THE KALE CHIPS: Place the kale on the prepared baking sheet. Add the olive oil and garlic, and season with salt and pepper. Gently toss to combine and arrange in a single layer. Bake for 10 to 13 minutes, or until crisp; let cool completely. Set aside.

c) FOR THE CRISPY BEANS: Using a clean kitchen towel or paper towels, dry the garbanzo beans thoroughly. Remove and discard skins. Place the garbanzos in a single layer on the baking sheet and bake for 20 minutes. Add the olive oil and chili lime seasoning and gently toss to combine. Bake until crisp and dry, an additional 15 to 17 minutes.

d) Turn off the oven and open the door slightly; cool completely in the oven for 1 hour.

e) Place the strawberries, grapes, and tangerines into meal prep containers. Will keep covered in the refrigerator 3 to 4 days. Kale chips and garbanzos should be kept separately in ziplock bags at room temperature to keep them nice and crisp.

48. Mini pumpkin protein donuts

Ingredients

- 1 cup white whole wheat flour
- $\frac{1}{2}$ cup vanilla whey protein powder
- $\frac{1}{3}$ cup firmly packed light brown sugar
- 1 $\frac{1}{2}$ teaspoons baking powder
- 1 teaspoon pumpkin pie spice
- $\frac{1}{4}$ teaspoon kosher salt
- 1 cup canned pumpkin puree
- 3 tablespoons unsalted butter, melted
- 2 large egg whites
- 2 tablespoons 2% milk
- 1 teaspoon ground cinnamon
- $\frac{1}{3}$ cup granulated sugar
- 2 tablespoons unsalted butter, melted

Directions

a) Preheat the oven to 350 degrees F. Coat the cups of the donut pan with nonstick spray.

b) In a large bowl, combine the flour, protein powder, brown sugar, baking powder, pumpkin pie spice, and salt.

c) In a large glass measuring cup or another bowl, whisk together the pumpkin, butter, egg whites, and milk.

d) Pour the wet mixture over the dry Ingredients and stir, using a rubber spatula, just until moist.

e) Scoop the batter evenly into the donut pan. Bake for 8 to 10 minutes, until the donuts are lightly browned and spring back when touched. Cool for 5 minutes.

f) Combine the cinnamon and sugar in a small bowl. Dip each donut into the melted butter and then into the cinnamon sugar.

g) Serve warm or at room temperature. Store in an airtight container up to 5 days.

49. Rainbow hummus veggie pinwheels

Ingredients

- 2 tablespoons hummus
- 1 (8-inch) spinach tortilla
- $\frac{1}{4}$ cup thinly sliced red bell pepper
- $\frac{1}{4}$ cup thinly sliced yellow bell pepper
- $\frac{1}{4}$ cup thinly sliced carrot
- $\frac{1}{4}$ cup thinly sliced cucumber
- $\frac{1}{4}$ cup baby spinach
- $\frac{1}{4}$ cup shredded red cabbage
- $\frac{1}{4}$ cup alfalfa sprouts
- $\frac{1}{2}$ cup strawberries
- $\frac{1}{2}$ cup blueberries

Directions

a) Spread the hummus over the surface of the tortilla in an even layer, leaving a $\frac{1}{4}$-inch border. Place the bell peppers, carrot, cucumber, spinach, cabbage, and sprouts in the center of the tortilla.

b) Bring the bottom edge of the tortilla tightly over the vegetables, folding in the sides. Continue rolling until the top of the tortilla is reached. Cut into sixths.

c) Place pinwheels, strawberries, and blueberries into a meal prep container. Refrigerate for 3 to 4 days.

50. Salsa snack box

Ingredients

- $\frac{3}{4}$ cup diced strawberries

- $\frac{3}{4}$ cup diced mango

- 1 jalapeño, seeded and minced

- 2 tablespoons diced red onion

- 2 tablespoons chopped fresh cilantro leaves

- 2 teaspoons honey

- Juice of 1 lime

- 2 cups tortilla chips

- 1 red bell pepper, thinly sliced

- 1 orange bell pepper, thinly sliced

- 1 jicama, peeled and sliced into thick matchsticks

- 1 pineapple, cut into wedges

Directions

a) In a large bowl, combine the strawberries, mango, jalapeño, onion, cilantro, honey, and lime juice.

b) Divide the tortilla chips into ziplock bags. Divide the salsa, bell peppers, jicama, and pineapple into meal prep containers. Will keep in the refrigerator 3 to 4 days.

51. Homemade Hummus

Yields about 2 cups

Ingredients

- 1 15 oz. can (425g) chickpeas, drained/rinsed (reserve liquid)
- $\frac{1}{4}$ cup (60mL) of the chickpea can liquid (or sub water)
- 1 Tablespoons minced garlic
- 1 Tablespoons tahini
- 1 $\frac{1}{2}$ Tablespoons lemon juice
- $\frac{1}{2}$ teaspoons cumin
- $\frac{1}{4}$ teaspoons salt
- $\frac{1}{4}$ teaspoons paprika
- $\frac{1}{8}$ teaspoons cayenne, to taste
- $\frac{1}{8}$ teaspoons pepper, to taste

Directions

a) Combine all ingredients in a food processor.

b) Scrape down the sides halfway through and adjust seasonings to taste.

52. Trail Mix

Yields about 2 cups

Ingredients

- 1 cup (15g) popped popcorn

- $\frac{1}{4}$ cup (40g) roasted peanuts

- $\frac{1}{4}$ cup (40g) roasted almonds

- $\frac{1}{4}$ cup (40g) pumpkin seeds

- $\frac{1}{4}$ cup (35g) dried blueberries, no added sugar

- 2 Tablespoons dark chocolate chips (optional)

- pinch of cinnamon (optional)

- pinch of salt

Directions

a) Toss all ingredients together, adjusting cinnamon and salt to taste if desired.

b) Store in an airtight container.

c) Lasts up to 2 weeks in the pantry.

53.Oil-Free Pesto

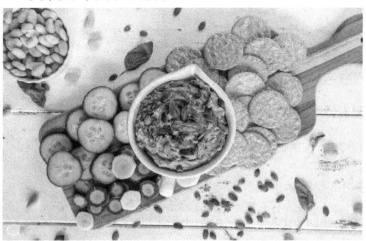

Yields about 2 cups

Ingredients

- 1 $\frac{1}{2}$ cups (60g) fresh basil

- 1 $\frac{1}{2}$ cups (60g) fresh spinach

- 1 15 oz. (425g) can white beans, drained/rinsed

- 2 Tablespoons walnuts

- 2 Tablespoons lemon juice

- 1 teaspoons garlic

- salt and pepper to taste

Directions

a) Place all ingredients in a food processor and process until well combined and desired consistency is reached.

b) Refrigerate after making.

c) Lasts 1-2 weeks in the fridge.

54.Egg Muffins

Yields about 12

Ingredients

- 3-4 cups (540-720g) mixed veggies, diced

- 2 cups (480g) of egg whites/substitute (or eggs), seasoned with salt and pepper

Directions

a) Preheat oven to 375F (190C).

b) Distribute mixed vegetables of your choice in sprayed muffin tin, filling up about ½ way.

c) Pour eggs into tins, filling ⅔ way to the top.

d) Bake for about 15 minutes, until completely set.

e) Enjoy warm or chill and enjoy cold! These are also great reheated.

f) Lasts about 3 days in the fridge, or 2-3 months in the freezer.

55. Tofu Bites

Yields 4 servings

Ingredients

- 1 14 oz. (400g) package extra firm tofu
- cooking spray
- salt and pepper
- additional seasoning

Directions

a) Preheat oven to 400F (200C).

b) Cut the pressed tofu into cubes or strips, as you prefer.

c) Toss lightly with a little cooking spray and seasonings, to taste. Transfer to a baking sheet lined with parchment paper.

d) Bake for about 45 minutes, turning halfway through.

56.Chicken Salad

Yields 1 serving

Ingredients

- 4 oz. (115g) chicken breast, shredded or cubed

- 2 Tablespoons Greek yogurt

- 1 teaspoons Dijon mustard

- 1 teaspoon yellow mustard

- 2 Tablespoons green onion

- 3 Tablespoons grapes, halved or quartered

- 3 Tablespoons chopped celery

- 2 Tablespoons chopped walnuts or pecans

- 1 teaspoons tarragon

- salt and pepper to taste

Directions

a) Mix all ingredients together.

b) Chill and enjoy! Lasts about 5 days in the fridge.

57.Tex-Mex Quinoa

Yields 12 servings

Ingredients

- 1 cup (180g) uncooked quinoa, rinsed

- 1 lb. (450g) extra lean ground turkey breast

- 1 15 oz. can (425g) black beans, drained/rinsed

- 1 15 oz. can (425g) sweet corn, drained/rinsed

- 1 10 oz. can (285g) diced tomatoes and green chiles

- 1 10 oz. can (285g) red enchilada sauce

- 1 $\frac{1}{2}$ cup (350mL) chicken/vegetable broth or water

- 1 green bell pepper, chopped $\frac{1}{2}$ cup (80g) chopped onion 2 jalapeño, seeded

- 1 Tablespoons minced garlic

- 2 Tablespoons taco seasoning

Directions

a) Add everything to the slow cooker. Stir well to combine.

b) Turn heat to low. Allow to cook for 6-8 hours, slow and low. Stir once or twice throughout the duration of the cooking time. (Cook on high for 4 hours if you're in a time crunch).

c) Serve with Greek yogurt as a sour cream substitute, salsa, and avocado or guacamole.

58. Tuna salad meal prep

Ingredients

- 2 large eggs
- 2 (5-ounce) cans tuna in water, drained and flaked
- $\frac{1}{2}$ cup non-fat Greek yogurt
- $\frac{1}{4}$ cup diced celery
- $\frac{1}{4}$ cup diced red onion
- 1 tablespoon Dijon mustard
- 1 tablespoon sweet pickle relish (optional)
- 1 teaspoon freshly squeezed lemon juice, or more to taste
- $\frac{1}{4}$ teaspoon garlic powder
- Kosher salt and freshly ground black pepper, to taste
- 4 Bibb lettuce leaves
- $\frac{1}{2}$ cup raw almonds
- 1 cucumber, sliced
- 1 apple, sliced

Directions

a) Place the eggs in a large saucepan and cover with cold water by 1 inch. Bring to a boil and cook for 1 minute. Cover the pot with a tight-fitting lid and remove from the heat; let sit for 8 to 10 minutes. Drain well and let cool before peeling and halving.

b) In a medium bowl, combine the tuna, yogurt, celery, onion, mustard, relish, lemon juice, and garlic powder; season with salt and pepper to taste.

c) Divide lettuce leaves into meal prep containers. Top with tuna mixture, and add the eggs, almonds, cucumber, and apple to the side. Will keep in the refrigerator 3 to 4 days.

WARM LUNCH

59.Chicken burrito bowls

Ingredients

Chipotle cream sauce

- ½ cup non-fat Greek yogurt
- 1 chipotle pepper in adobo sauce, minced, or more to taste
- 1 clove garlic, minced
- 1 tablespoon freshly squeezed lime juice

Burrito Bowl

- ⅔ cup brown rice
- 1 tablespoon olive oil
- 1-pound ground chicken
- ½ teaspoon chili powder
- ½ teaspoon garlic powder
- ½ teaspoon ground cumin
- ½ teaspoon dried oregano
- ¼ teaspoon onion powder
- ¼ teaspoon paprika
- Kosher salt and freshly ground black pepper, to taste

- 1 (15-ounce) can black beans, drained and rinsed

- 1 ¾ cups corn kernels (frozen, canned, or roasted)

- ½ cup pico de gallo (homemade or store-bought)

Directions

a) FOR THE CHIPOTLE CREAM SAUCE: Whisk together the yogurt, chipotle pepper, garlic, and lime juice. Cover and refrigerate for up to 3 days.

b) Cook the rice according to package instructions in a large saucepan with 2 cups water; set aside.

c) Heat the olive oil in a large stockpot or Dutch oven over medium-high heat. Add the ground chicken, chili powder, garlic powder, cumin, oregano, onion powder, and paprika; season with salt and pepper. Cook until the chicken has browned, 3 to 5 minutes, making sure to crumble the chicken as it cooks; drain excess fat.

d) Divide rice into meal prep containers. Top with ground chicken mixture, black beans, corn, and pico de gallo. Will keep covered in the refrigerator for 3 to 4 days. Drizzle with chipotle cream sauce. Garnish with cilantro and lime wedge, if desired, and serve. Reheat in the microwave in 30-second intervals until heated through.

60.Chicken tikka masala

Ingredients

- 1 cup basmati rice

- 2 tablespoons unsalted butter

- 1 $\frac{1}{2}$ pounds boneless, skinless chicken breasts, cut into 1-inch chunks

- Kosher salt and freshly ground black pepper, to taste

- 1 onion, diced

- 2 tablespoons tomato paste

- 1 tablespoon freshly grated ginger

- 3 cloves garlic, minced

- 2 teaspoons garam masala

- 2 teaspoons chili powder

- 2 teaspoons ground turmeric

- 1 (28-ounce) can diced tomatoes

- 1 cup chicken stock

- $\frac{1}{3}$ cup heavy cream

- 1 tablespoon fresh lemon juice

- $\frac{1}{4}$ cup chopped fresh cilantro leaves (optional)

- 1 lemon, cut into wedges (optional)

Directions

a) Cook the rice according to package instructions in a large saucepan with 2 cups water; set aside.

b) Melt the butter in a large skillet over medium heat. Season the chicken with salt and pepper. Add the chicken and onion to the skillet and cook, stirring occasionally, until golden, 4 to 5 minutes. Stir in the tomato paste, ginger, garlic, garam masala, chili powder, and turmeric and cook until well combined, 1 to 2 minutes. Stir in the diced tomatoes and chicken stock. Bring to a boil; reduce the heat and simmer, stirring occasionally, until slightly thickened, about 10 minutes.

c) Stir in the cream, lemon juice, and chicken and cook until heated through, about 1 minute.

d) Place the rice and chicken mixture into meal prep containers. Garnish with cilantro and lemon wedge, if desired, and serve. Will keep covered in the refrigerator 3 to 4 days. Reheat in the microwave in 30-second intervals until heated through.

61.Greek chicken bowls

Ingredients

Chicken and rice

- 1 pound boneless, skinless chicken breasts

- $\frac{1}{4}$ cup plus 2 tablespoons olive oil, divided

- 3 cloves garlic, minced

- Juice of 1 lemon

- 1 tablespoon red wine vinegar

- 1 tablespoon dried oregano

- Kosher salt and freshly ground black pepper, to taste

- $\frac{3}{4}$ cup brown rice

Cucumber salad

- 2 English cucumbers, peeled and sliced

- $\frac{1}{2}$ cup thinly sliced red onion

- Juice of 1 lemon

- 2 tablespoons extra-virgin olive oil

- 1 tablespoon red wine vinegar

- 2 cloves garlic, pressed

- ½ teaspoon dried oregano

Tzatziki sauce

- 1 cup Greek yogurt

- 1 English cucumber, finely diced

- 2 cloves garlic, pressed

- 1 tablespoon chopped fresh dill

- 1 teaspoon grated lemon zest

- 1 tablespoon freshly squeezed lemon juice

- 1 teaspoon chopped fresh mint (optional)

- Kosher salt and freshly ground black pepper, to taste

- 2 tablespoons extra-virgin olive oil

- 1 ½ pounds cherry tomatoes, halved

Directions

a) FOR THE CHICKEN: In a gallon-size ziplock bag, combine the chicken, ¼ cup of the olive oil, the garlic, lemon juice, vinegar, and oregano; season with salt and pepper. Marinate the chicken in the refrigerator for at least 20 minutes or up to 1 hour, turning the bag occasionally. Drain the chicken and discard the marinade.

b) Heat the remaining 2 tablespoons olive oil in a large skillet over medium-high heat. Add the chicken and cook, flipping once, until cooked through, 3 to 4 minutes per side. Let cool before dicing into bite-size pieces.

c) Cook the rice in a large saucepan with 2 cups water according to package instructions.

d) Divide the rice and chicken into meal prep containers. Will keep covered in the refrigerator up to 3 days.

e) FOR THE CUCUMBER SALAD: Combine the cucumbers, onion, lemon juice, olive oil, vinegar, garlic, and oregano in a small bowl. Cover and refrigerate for up to 3 days.

f) FOR THE TZATZIKI SAUCE: Combine the yogurt, cucumber, garlic, dill, lemon zest and juice, and mint (if using) in a small bowl. Season with salt and pepper to taste and drizzle with the olive oil. Cover and refrigerate for at least 10 minutes, allowing the flavors to meld. Can be refrigerated 3 to 4 days.

g) To serve, reheat rice and chicken in the microwave in 30-second intervals, until heated through. Top with cucumber salad, tomatoes, and Tzatziki sauce and serve.

62.Korean meal prep beef bowls

Ingredients

- ⅔ cup white or brown rice

- 4 medium eggs

- 1 tablespoon olive oil

- 2 cloves garlic, minced

- 4 cups chopped spinach

Korean beef

- 3 tablespoons packed brown sugar

- 3 tablespoons reduced-sodium soy sauce

- 1 tablespoon freshly grated ginger

- 1 ½ teaspoons sesame oil

- ½ teaspoon sriracha (optional)

- 2 teaspoons olive oil

- 2 cloves garlic, minced

- 1-pound ground beef

- 2 green onions, thinly sliced (optional)

- ¼ teaspoon sesame seeds (optional)

Directions

a) Cook the rice according to package instructions; set aside.

b) Place the eggs in a large saucepan and cover with cold water by 1 inch. Bring to a boil and cook for 1 minute. Cover the pot with a tight-fitting lid and remove from the heat; let sit for 8 to 10 minutes. Drain well and let cool before peeling and slicing in half.

c) Heat the olive oil in a large skillet over medium-high heat. Add the garlic and cook, stirring frequently, until fragrant, 1 to 2 minutes. Stir in the spinach and cook until wilted, 2 to 3 minutes; set aside.

d) For the beef: In a small bowl, whisk together the brown sugar, soy sauce, ginger, sesame oil, and sriracha, if using.

e) Heat the olive oil in a large skillet over medium-high heat. Add the garlic and cook, stirring constantly, until fragrant, about 1 minute. Add the ground beef and cook until browned, 3 to 5 minutes, making sure to crumble the beef as it cooks; drain excess fat. Stir in the soy sauce mixture and the green onions until well combined, then simmer until heated through, about 2 minutes.

f) Place rice, eggs, spinach, and ground beef mixture into meal prep containers and garnish with green onion and sesame seeds, if desired. Will keep covered in the refrigerator 3 to 4 days.

g) Reheat in the microwave in 30-second intervals until heated through.

63. Mason jar chicken and ramen soup

Ingredients

- 2 (5.6-ounce) packages refrigerated yakisoba noodles

- 2 $\frac{1}{2}$ tablespoons reduced-sodium vegetable broth base concentrate (we like Better Than Bouillon)

- 1 $\frac{1}{2}$ tablespoons reduced-sodium soy sauce

- 1 tablespoon rice wine vinegar

- 1 tablespoon freshly grated ginger

- 2 teaspoons sambal oelek (ground fresh chile paste), or more to taste

- 2 teaspoons sesame oil

- 2 cups leftover shredded rotisserie chicken

- 3 cups baby spinach

- 2 carrots, peeled and grated

- 1 cup sliced shiitake mushrooms

- $\frac{1}{2}$ cup fresh cilantro leaves

- 2 green onions, thinly sliced

- 1 teaspoon sesame seeds

Directions

a) In a large pot of boiling water, cook the yakisoba until loosened, 1 to 2 minutes; drain well.

b) In a small bowl, combine the broth base, soy sauce, vinegar, ginger, sambal oelek, and sesame oil.

c) Divide the broth mixture into 4 (24-ounce) wide-mouth glass jars with lids, or other heatproof containers. Top with yakisoba, chicken, spinach, carrots, mushrooms, cilantro, green onions, and sesame seeds. Cover and refrigerate for up to 4 days.

d) To serve, uncover a jar and add enough hot water to cover the contents, about 1 $\frac{1}{4}$ cups. Microwave, uncovered, until heated through, 2 to 3 minutes. Let stand 5 minutes, stir to combine, and serve immediately.

64. Mason jar bolognese

Ingredients

- 2 tablespoons olive oil

- 1-pound ground beef

- 1 pound Italian sausage, casings removed

- 1 onion, minced

- 4 cloves garlic, minced

- 3 (14.5-ounce) cans diced tomatoes, drained

- 2 (15-ounce) cans tomato sauce

- 3 bay leaves

- 1 teaspoon dried oregano

- 1 teaspoon dried basil

- $\frac{1}{2}$ teaspoon dried thyme

- 1 teaspoon kosher salt

- $\frac{1}{2}$ teaspoon freshly ground black pepper

- 2 (16-ounce) packages reduced-fat mozzarella cheese, cubed

- 32 ounces uncooked whole wheat fusilli, cooked according to package instructions; about 16 cups cooked

Directions

a) Heat the olive oil in a large skillet over medium-high heat. Add the ground beef, sausage, onion, and garlic. Cook until browned, 5 to 7 minutes, making sure to crumble the beef and sausage as it cooks; drain excess fat.

b) Transfer the ground beef mixture to a 6-quart slow cooker. Stir in the tomatoes, tomato sauce, bay leaves, oregano, basil, thyme, salt, and pepper. Cover and cook on low heat for 7 hours and 45 minutes. Remove the lid and turn the slow cooker to high. Continue to cook for 15 minutes, until the sauce has thickened. Discard the bay leaves and let the sauce cool completely.

c) Divide sauce into 16 (24-ounce) wide-mouth glass jars with lids, or other heatproof containers. Top with mozzarella and fusilli. Refrigerate for up to 4 days.

d) To serve, microwave, uncovered, until heated through, about 2 minutes. Stir to combine.

65. Mason jar lasagna

Ingredients

- 3 lasagna noodles
- 1 tablespoon olive oil
- ½ pound ground sirloin
- 1 onion, diced
- 2 cloves garlic, minced
- 3 tablespoons tomato paste
- 1 teaspoon Italian seasoning
- 2 (14.5-ounce) cans diced tomatoes
- 1 medium zucchini, grated
- 1 large carrot, grated
- 2 cups shredded baby spinach
- Kosher salt and freshly ground black pepper, to taste
- 1 cup part-skim ricotta cheese
- 1 cup shredded mozzarella cheese, divided
- 2 tablespoons chopped fresh basil leaves

Directions

a) In a large pot of boiling salted water, cook the pasta according to package instructions; drain well. Cut each noodle into 4 pieces; set aside.

b) Heat the olive oil in a large skillet or Dutch oven over medium-high heat. Add the ground sirloin and onion and cook until browned, 3 to 5 minutes, making sure to crumble the beef as it cooks; drain excess fat.

c) Stir in the garlic, tomato paste, and Italian seasoning and cook until fragrant, 1 to 2 minutes. Stir in the tomatoes, reduce the heat, and simmer until slightly thickened, 5 to 6 minutes. Stir in the zucchini, carrot, and spinach and cook, stirring frequently, until tender, 2 to 3 minutes. Season with salt and pepper to taste. Set sauce aside.

d) In a small bowl, combine the ricotta, $\frac{1}{2}$ cup of the mozzarella, and the basil; season with salt and pepper to taste

e) Preheat the oven to 375 degrees F. Lightly oil 4 (16-ounce) wide-mouth glass jars with lids, or other oven-safe containers, or coat with nonstick spray.

f) Place 1 pasta piece into each jar. Divide one-third of the sauce into the jars. Repeat with a second layer of pasta and sauce. Top with ricotta mixture, remaining pasta, and remaining sauce. Sprinkle with remaining $\frac{1}{2}$ cup mozzarella cheese.

g) Set the jars on a baking sheet. Place in the oven and bake until bubbling, 25 to 30 minutes; cool completely. Refrigerate for up to 4 days.

66. Miso ginger detox soup

Ingredients

- 2 teaspoons toasted sesame oil

- 2 teaspoons canola oil

- 3 cloves garlic, minced

- 1 tablespoon freshly grated ginger

- 6 cups vegetable stock

- 1 sheet kombu, cut into small pieces

- 4 teaspoons white miso paste

- 1 (3.5-ounce) package shiitake mushrooms, sliced (about 2 cups)

- 8 ounces' firm tofu, cubed

- 5 baby bok choy, chopped

- $\frac{1}{4}$ cup sliced green onions

Directions

a) Heat the sesame oil and canola oil in a large stockpot or Dutch oven over medium heat. Add the garlic and ginger and cook, stirring frequently, until fragrant, 1 to 2 minutes. Stir in the stock, kombu, and miso paste and bring to a boil. Cover, reduce the heat, and simmer for 10 minutes. Stir in the mushrooms and cook until tender, about 5 minutes.

b) Stir in the tofu and bok choy and cook until the tofu is heated through and the bok choy is just tender, about 2 minutes. Stir in the green onions. Serve immediately.

c) Or, to prep ahead of time, let the stock cool completely at the end of step 1. Then stir in the tofu, bok choy, and green onions. Divide into airtight containers, cover, and refrigerate for up to 3 days. To reheat, place in the microwave in 30-second intervals until heated through.

67.Stuffed sweet potatoes

YIELD: 4 SERVINGS

Ingredients

- 4 medium sweet potatoes

Directions

a) Preheat the oven to 400 degrees F. Line a baking sheet with parchment paper or aluminum foil.

b) Place the sweet potatoes in a single layer on the prepared baking sheet. Bake until fork-tender, about 1 hour and 10 minutes.

c) Let rest until cool enough to handle.

68.Korean Chicken Stuffed Potatoes

Ingredients

- ½ cup seasoned rice wine vinegar

- 1 tablespoon sugar

- Kosher salt and freshly ground black pepper, to taste

- 1 cup matchstick carrots

- 1 large shallot, sliced

- ¼ teaspoon crushed red pepper flakes

- 2 teaspoons sesame oil

- 1 (10-ounce) package fresh spinach

- 2 cloves garlic, minced

- 4 roasted sweet potatoes (here)

- 2 cups Spicy Korean Sesame Chicken (here)

Directions

a) In a small saucepan, combine the vinegar, sugar, 1 teaspoon salt, and $\frac{1}{4}$ cup water. Bring to a boil over medium heat. Stir in the carrots, shallot, and red pepper flakes. Remove from the heat and let stand 30 minutes.

b) Heat the sesame oil in a large skillet over medium heat. Stir in the spinach and garlic and cook until the spinach has wilted, 2 to 4 minutes. Season with salt and pepper to taste.

c) Halve the potatoes lengthwise and season with salt and pepper. Top with the chicken, carrot mixture, and spinach.

d) Divide the sweet potatoes into meal prep containers. Refrigerate for up to 3 days. Reheat in the microwave in 30-second intervals until heated through.

69.Kale and Red Pepper Stuffed Potatoes

Ingredients

- 1 tablespoon olive oil

- 2 cloves garlic, minced

- 1 sweet onion, diced

- 1 teaspoon smoked paprika

- 1 red bell pepper, thinly sliced

- 1 bunch curly kale, stems removed and leaves chopped

- Kosher salt and freshly ground black pepper, to taste

- 4 roasted sweet potatoes

- ½ cup crumbled reduced-fat feta cheese

Directions

a) Heat the olive oil in a large skillet over medium heat. Add the garlic and onion and cook, stirring frequently, until the onion is translucent, 2 to 3 minutes. Stir in the paprika and cook until fragrant, about 30 seconds.

b) Stir in the bell pepper and cook until crisp-tender, about 2 minutes. Stir in the kale, a handful at a time, and cook until bright green and just wilted, 3 to 4 minutes.

c) Halve potatoes and season with salt and pepper. Top with the kale mixture and feta.

d) Divide the sweet potatoes into meal prep containers.

70.Mustard Chicken Stuffed Potatoes

Ingredients

- 1 tablespoon olive oil

- 2 cups cut fresh green beans

- 1 $\frac{1}{2}$ cups quartered cremini mushrooms

- 1 shallot, minced

- 1 clove garlic, minced

- 2 tablespoons chopped fresh parsley leaves

- Kosher salt and freshly ground black pepper, to taste

- 4 roasted sweet potatoes (here)

- 2 cups Honey Mustard Chicken (here)

Directions

a) Heat the olive oil in a large skillet over medium heat. Add the green beans, mushrooms, and shallot and cook, stirring frequently, until the green beans are crisp-tender, 5 to 6 minutes. Stir in the garlic and parsley and cook until fragrant, about 1 minute. Season with salt and pepper to taste.

b) Halve the potatoes lengthwise and season with salt and pepper. Top with the green bean mixture and chicken.

c) Divide the sweet potatoes into meal prep containers. Refrigerate for up to 3 days. Reheat in the microwave in 30-second intervals until heated through.

71.Black Bean and Pico de Gallo Stuffed Potatoes

Ingredients

Black beans

- 1 tablespoon olive oil
- ½ sweet onion, diced
- 1 clove garlic, minced
- 1 teaspoon chili powder
- ½ teaspoon ground cumin
- 1 (15.5-ounce) can black beans, rinsed and drained
- 1 teaspoon apple cider vinegar
- Kosher salt and freshly ground black pepper, to taste

Pico de gallo

- 2 plum tomatoes, diced
- ½ sweet onion, diced
- 1 jalapeño, seeded and minced
- 3 tablespoons chopped fresh cilantro leaves
- 1 tablespoon freshly squeezed lime juice
- Kosher salt and freshly ground black pepper, to taste

- 4 roasted sweet potatoes (here)

- 1 avocado, halved, pitted, peeled, and diced

- ¼ cup light sour cream

Directions

a) FOR THE BEANS: Heat the olive oil in a medium saucepan over medium heat. Add the onion and cook, stirring frequently, until translucent, 2 to 3 minutes. Stir in the garlic, chili powder, and cumin and cook until fragrant, about 1 minute.

b) Stir in the beans and ⅔ cup water. Bring to a simmer, reduce the heat, and cook until reduced, 10 to 15 minutes. Using a potato masher, mash the beans until smooth and desired consistency is reached. Stir in the vinegar and season with salt and pepper to taste.

c) FOR THE PICO DE GALLO: Combine the tomatoes, onion, jalapeño, cilantro, and lime juice in a medium bowl. Season with salt and pepper to taste.

d) Halve the potatoes lengthwise and season with salt and pepper. Top with the black bean mixture and pico de gallo.

e) Divide the sweet potatoes into meal prep containers. Refrigerate for up to 3 days. Reheat in the microwave in 30-second intervals until heated through.

72.Zucchini noodles with turkey meatballs

Ingredients

- 1-pound ground turkey
- ⅓ cup panko
- 3 tablespoons freshly grated Parmesan
- 2 large egg yolks
- ¾ teaspoon dried oregano
- ¾ teaspoon dried basil
- ½ teaspoon dried parsley
- ¼ teaspoon garlic powder
- ¼ teaspoon crushed red pepper flakes
- Kosher salt and freshly ground black pepper, to taste
- 2 pounds (3 medium) zucchini, spiralized
- 2 teaspoons kosher salt
- 2 cups marinara sauce (homemade or store-bought)
- ¼ cup freshly grated Parmesan cheese

Directions

a) Preheat the oven to 400 degrees F. Lightly oil a 9x13-inch baking dish or coat with nonstick spray.

b) In a large bowl, combine the ground turkey, panko, Parmesan, egg yolks, oregano, basil, parsley, garlic powder, and red pepper flakes; season with salt and pepper. Using a wooden spoon or clean hands, mix until well combined. Roll the mixture into 16 to 20 meatballs, each 1 to 1 $\frac{1}{2}$ inches in diameter.

c) Place the meatballs in the prepared baking dish and bake for 15 to 18 minutes, until browned all over and cooked through; set aside.

d) Place the zucchini in a colander over the sink. Add the salt and gently toss to combine; let sit for 10 minutes. In a large pot of boiling water, cook the zucchini for 30 seconds to 1 minute; drain well.

e) Divide the zucchini into meal prep containers. Top with meatballs, marinara sauce, and Parmesan. Will keep covered in the refrigerator 3 to 4 days. Reheat in the microwave, uncovered, in 30-second intervals until heated through.

73. Easy Meatballs

Yields about 18 meatballs

Ingredients

- 20 oz. (600g) extra lean ground turkey breast

- ½ cup (40g) oat flour

- 1 egg

- 2 cups (80g) spinach, chopped (optional)

- 1 teaspoons garlic powder

- ¾ teaspoons salt

- ½ teaspoons pepper

Directions

a) Preheat oven to 350F (180C).

b) Mix all ingredients in a bowl.

c) Roll meat into golf ball sized meatballs and transfer to a sprayed 9x13" (30x20cm) baking dish.

d) Bake for 15 minutes.

74.3-Ingredient Soup

Yields 8 servings

Ingredients

- 2 15 oz. (425g each) cans of beans (I use one can of black beans and one can of white beans), drained/rinsed

- 1 15 oz. (425g) can diced tomatoes

- 1 cup (235mL) chicken/vegetable broth salt and pepper to taste

Directions

a) Combine all ingredients in a saucepan over medium-high heat. Bring to a boil.

b) Once boiling, cover and turn down to a simmer for 25 minutes.

c) Use your immersion blender (or transfer to a normal blender/processor in batches) to puree the soup to your desired consistency.

d) Serve warm with Greek yogurt as a sour cream substitute, low fat cheddar cheese and green onion!

e) Lasts up to 5 days in the fridge.

75.Slow Cooker Salsa Turkey

Yields 6 servings

Ingredients

- 20 oz. (600g) extra lean ground turkey breast

- 1 15.5 oz. jar (440g) of salsa

- salt and pepper to taste (optional)

Directions

a) Add your ground turkey and salsa to your slow cooker.

b) Turn heat to low. Allow to cook for 6-8 hours, slow and low. Stir once or twice throughout the duration of the cooking time. (Cook on high for 4 hours if you're in a time crunch).

c) Serve with additional cold salsa, Greek yogurt as a sour cream substitute, cheese or green onion!

d) Lasts 5 days in the fridge, or 3-4 months in the freezer.

76. Burrito-Bowl-In-A-Jar

Yields 1 Jar

Ingredients

- 2 Tablespoons salsa

- $\frac{1}{4}$ cup (40g) beans/bean salsa $\frac{1}{3}$ cup (60g) cooked rice/quinoa

- 3 oz. (85g) cooked extra lean ground turkey, chicken, or protein of choice

- 2 Tablespoons low fat cheddar cheese

- 1 $\frac{1}{2}$ cups (60g) lettuce/greens

- 1 Tablespoons Greek yogurt ("sour cream")

- $\frac{1}{4}$ avocado

Directions

a) Layer all of your Ingredients into the jar.

b) Store for eating at a later time.

c) When ready to eat, pour the jar onto a plate or bowl to mix up and devour!

d) Lasts 4-5 days in the fridge.

COLD LUNCH

77.Carnitas meal prep bowls

Ingredients

- 2 ½ teaspoons chili powder

- 1 ½ teaspoons ground cumin

- 1 ½ teaspoons dried oregano

- 1 teaspoon kosher salt, or more to taste

- ½ teaspoon ground black pepper, or more to taste

- 1 (3-pound) pork loin, excess fat trimmed

- 4 cloves garlic, peeled

- 1 onion, cut into wedges

- Juice of 2 oranges

- Juice of 2 limes

- 8 cups shredded kale

- 4 plum tomatoes, chopped

- 2 (15-ounce) cans black beans, drained and rinsed

- 4 cups corn kernels (frozen, canned, or roasted)

- 2 avocados, halved, pitted, peeled, and diced

- 2 limes, cut into wedges

Directions

a) In a small bowl, combine the chili powder, cumin, oregano, salt, and pepper. Season the pork with the spice mixture, rubbing in thoroughly on all sides.

b) Place the pork, garlic, onion, orange juice, and lime juice in a slow cooker. Cover and cook on low for 8 hours, or on high for 4 to 5 hours.

c) Remove the pork from the cooker and shred the meat. Return it to the pot and toss with the juices; season with salt and pepper, if needed. Cover and keep warm for an additional 30 minutes.

d) Place the pork, kale, tomatoes, black beans, and corn into meal prep containers. Will keep covered in the refrigerator 3 to 4 days. Serve with avocado and lime wedges.

78. Chicago hot dog salad

Ingredients

- 2 tablespoons extra-virgin olive oil
- 1 ½ tablespoons yellow mustard
- 1 tablespoon red wine vinegar
- 2 teaspoons poppy seeds
- ½ teaspoon celery salt
- Pinch of sugar
- Kosher salt and freshly ground black pepper, to taste
- 1 cup quinoa
- 4 reduced-fat turkey hot dogs
- 3 cups shredded baby kale
- 1 cup halved cherry tomatoes
- ⅓ cup diced white onion
- ¼ cup sport peppers
- 8 dill pickle spears

Directions

a) TO MAKE THE VINAIGRETTE: Whisk together the olive oil, mustard, vinegar, poppy seeds, celery salt, and sugar in a medium bowl. Season with salt and pepper to taste. Cover and refrigerate for 3 to 4 days.

b) Cook the quinoa according to package instructions in a large saucepan with 2 cups water; set aside.

c) Heat a grill to medium-high. Add the hot dogs to the grill and cook until golden brown and lightly charred on all sides, 4 to 5 minutes. Let cool and cut into bite-size pieces.

d) Divide the quinoa, hot dogs, tomatoes, onion, and peppers into meal prep containers. Will keep refrigerated 3 to 4 days.

e) To serve, pour the dressing on top of the salad and gently toss to combine. Serve immediately, garnished with pickle spears, if desired.

79.Fish taco bowls

Ingredients

Cilantro lime dressing

- 1 cup loosely packed cilantro, stems removed

- ½ cup Greek yogurt

- 2 cloves garlic,

- Juice of 1 lime

- Pinch of kosher salt

- ¼ cup extra-virgin olive oil

- 2 tablespoons apple cider vinegar

Tilapia

- 3 tablespoons unsalted butter, melted

- 3 cloves garlic, minced

- Grated zest of 1 lime

- 2 tablespoons freshly squeezed lime juice, or more to taste

- 4 (4-ounce) tilapia fillets

- Kosher salt and freshly ground black pepper, to taste

- ⅔ cup quinoa

- 2 cups shredded kale

- 1 cup shredded red cabbage

- 1 cup corn kernels (canned or roasted)

- 2 plum tomatoes, diced

- $\frac{1}{4}$ cup crushed tortilla chips

- 2 tablespoons chopped fresh cilantro leaves

Directions

a) FOR THE DRESSING: Combine the cilantro, yogurt, garlic, lime juice, and salt in the bowl of a food processor. With the motor running, add the olive oil and vinegar in a slow stream until emulsified. Cover and refrigerate for 3 to 4 days.

b) FOR THE TILAPIA: Preheat the oven to 425 degrees F. Lightly oil a 9x13-inch baking dish or coat with nonstick spray.

c) In a small bowl, whisk together the butter, garlic, lime zest, and lime juice. Season the tilapia with salt and pepper and place in the prepared baking dish. Drizzle with the butter mixture.

d) Bake until the fish flakes easily with a fork, 10 to 12 minutes.

e) Cook the quinoa according to package instructions in a large saucepan with 2 cups water. Let cool.

f) Divide the quinoa into meal prep containers. Top with tilapia, kale, cabbage, corn, tomatoes, and tortilla chips.

g) To serve, drizzle with cilantro lime dressing, garnished with cilantro, if desired.

80. Harvest cobb salad

Ingredients

Poppy seed dressing

- ¼ cup 2% milk

- 3 tablespoons olive oil mayonnaise

- 2 tablespoons Greek yogurt

- 1 ½ tablespoons sugar, or more to taste

- 1 tablespoon apple cider vinegar

- 1 tablespoon poppy seeds

- 2 tablespoons olive oil

Salad

- 16 ounces' butternut squash, cut into 1-inch chunks

- 16 ounces Brussels sprouts, halved

- 2 sprigs fresh thyme

- 5 fresh sage leaves

- Kosher salt and freshly ground black pepper, to taste

- 4 medium eggs

- 4 slices bacon, diced

- 8 cups shredded kale

- 1 ⅓ cups cooked wild rice

Directions

a) FOR THE DRESSING: Whisk together the milk, mayonnaise, yogurt, sugar, vinegar, and poppy seeds in a small bowl. Cover and refrigerate for up to 3 days.

b) Preheat the oven to 400 degrees F. Lightly oil a baking sheet or coat with nonstick spray.

c) Place the squash and Brussels sprouts on the prepared baking sheet. Add the olive oil, thyme, and sage and gently toss to combine; season with salt and pepper. Arrange in an even layer and bake, turning once, for 25 to 30 minutes, until tender; set aside.

d) Meanwhile, place the eggs in a large saucepan and cover with cold water by 1 inch. Bring to a boil and cook for 1 minute. Cover the pot with a tight-fitting lid and remove from heat; let sit for 8 to 10 minutes. Drain well and let cool before peeling and slicing.

e) Heat a large skillet over medium-high heat. Add the bacon and cook until brown and crispy, 6 to 8 minutes; drain excess fat. Transfer to a paper towel-lined plate; set aside.

f) To assemble the salads, place the kale into meal prep containers; arrange rows of squash, Brussels sprouts, bacon, egg, and wild rice on top. Will keep covered in the refrigerator 3 to 4 days. Serve with the poppy seed dressing.

81.Buffalo cauliflower cobb salad

Ingredients

- 3-4 cups cauliflower florets
- 1 15 oz. can chickpeas, drained, rinsed and patted dry
- 2 teaspoons avocado oil
- $\frac{1}{2}$ teaspoon pepper
- $\frac{1}{2}$ teaspoon sea salt
- $\frac{1}{2}$ cup buffalo wing sauce
- 4 cups fresh romaine, chopped
- $\frac{1}{2}$ cup celery, chopped
- $\frac{1}{4}$ cup red onion, sliced
- Creamy Vegan Ranch Dressing:
- $\frac{1}{2}$ cup raw cashews, soaked 3-4 hours or overnight
- $\frac{1}{2}$ cup fresh water
- 2 teaspoons dried dill
- 1 teaspoon garlic powder
- 1 teaspoon onion powder
- $\frac{1}{2}$ teaspoon sea salt
- pinch of black pepper

Directions

a) Set oven to 450°F.

b) Add cauliflower, chickpeas, oil, pepper and salt to large bowl and toss to coat.

c) Pour mixture onto a baking sheet or stone. Roast for 20 minutes. Remove baking sheet from the oven, pour buffalo sauce over the mixture and toss to coat. Roast for another 10-15 minutes or until chickpeas are crispy and cauliflower is roasted to your liking. Remove from oven.

d) Add soaked and drained cashews into a high powered blender or food processor with 1/2 cup water, dill, garlic powder, onion powder, salt and pepper. Blend until smooth.

e) Grab two salad bowls and the add 2 cups of chopped romaine, 1/4 cup celery and 1/8 cup of onion to each bowl. Top with roasted buffalo cauliflower and chickpeas. Drizzle on dressing and enjoy!

82.Mason jar beet and brussels sprout grain bowls

Ingredients

- 3 medium beets (about 1 pound)
- 1 tablespoon olive oil
- Kosher salt and freshly ground black pepper, to taste
- 1 cup farro
- 4 cups baby spinach or kale
- 2 cups Brussels sprouts (about 8 ounces), thinly sliced
- 3 clementines, peeled and segmented
- $\frac{1}{2}$ cup pecans, toasted
- $\frac{1}{2}$ cup pomegranate seeds

Honey-Dijon red wine vinaigrette

- $\frac{1}{4}$ cup extra-virgin olive oil
- 2 tablespoons red wine vinegar
- $\frac{1}{2}$ shallot, minced
- 1 tablespoon honey
- 2 teaspoons whole grain mustard
- Kosher salt and freshly ground black pepper, to taste

Directions

a) Preheat the oven to 400 degrees F. Line a baking sheet with foil.

b) Place the beets on the foil, drizzle with olive oil, and season with salt and pepper. Fold up all 4 sides of the foil to make a pouch. Bake until fork-tender, 35 to 45 minutes; let cool, about 30 minutes.

c) Using a clean paper towel, rub the beets to remove the skins; dice into bite-size pieces.

d) Cook the farro according to package Directions, then let cool.

e) Divide the beets into 4 (32-ounce) wide-mouth glass jars with lids. Top with spinach or kale, farro, Brussels sprouts, clementines, pecans, and pomegranate seeds. Will keep covered in the refrigerator 3 or 4 days.

f) FOR THE VINAIGRETTE: Whisk together the olive oil, vinegar, shallot, honey, mustard, and 1 tablespoon water; season with salt and pepper to taste. Cover and refrigerate for up to 3 days.

g) To serve, add the vinaigrette to each jar and shake. Serve immediately.

83.Mason jar broccoli salad

Ingredients

- 3 tablespoons 2% milk

- 2 tablespoons olive oil mayonnaise

- 2 tablespoons Greek yogurt

- 1 tablespoon sugar, or more to taste

- 2 teaspoons apple cider vinegar

- $\frac{1}{2}$ cup cashews

- $\frac{1}{4}$ cup dried cranberries

- $\frac{1}{2}$ cup diced red onion

- 2 ounces' cheddar cheese, diced

- 5 cups coarsely chopped broccoli florets

Directions

a) FOR THE DRESSING: Whisk together the milk, mayonnaise, yogurt, sugar, and vinegar in a small bowl.

b) Divide the dressing into 4 (16-ounce) wide-mouth glass jars with lids. Top with cashews, cranberries, onion, cheese, and broccoli. Refrigerate for up to 3 days.

c) To serve, shake the contents of a jar and serve immediately.

84. Mason jar chicken salad

Ingredients

- 2 ½ cups leftover shredded rotisserie chicken

- ½ cup Greek yogurt

- 2 tablespoons olive oil mayonnaise

- ¼ cup diced red onion

- 1 stalk celery, diced

- 1 tablespoon freshly squeezed lemon juice, or more to taste

- 1 teaspoon chopped fresh tarragon

- ½ teaspoon Dijon mustard

- ½ teaspoon garlic powder

- Kosher salt and freshly ground black pepper, to taste

- 4 cups shredded kale

- 2 Granny Smith apples, cored and chopped

- ½ cup cashews

- ½ cup dried cranberries

Directions

a) In a large bowl, combine the chicken, yogurt, mayonnaise, red onion, celery, lemon juice, tarragon, mustard, and garlic powder; season with salt and pepper to taste.

b) Divide the chicken mixture into 4 (24-ounce) wide-mouth glass jars with lids. Top with kale, apples, cashews, and cranberries. Refrigerate for up to 3 days.

c) To serve, shake contents of a jar and serve immediately.

85.Mason jar Chinese chicken salad

Ingredients

- ½ cup rice wine vinegar

- 2 cloves garlic, pressed

- 1 tablespoon sesame oil

- 1 tablespoon freshly grated ginger

- 2 teaspoons sugar, or more to taste

- ½ teaspoon reduced-sodium soy sauce

- 2 green onions, thinly sliced

- 1 teaspoon sesame seeds

- 2 carrots, peeled and grated

- 2 cups diced English cucumber

- 2 cups shredded purple cabbage

- 12 cups chopped kale

- 1 ½ cups leftover diced rotisserie chicken

- 1 cup wonton strips

Directions

a) FOR THE VINAIGRETTE: Whisk together the vinegar, garlic, sesame oil, ginger, sugar, and soy sauce in a small bowl. Divide the dressing into 4 (32-ounce) wide-mouth glass jars with lids.

b) Top with green onions, sesame seeds, carrots, cucumber, cabbage, kale, and chicken. Refrigerate for up to 3 days. Store the wonton strips separately.

c) To serve, shake contents of a jar and add the wonton strips. Serve immediately.

86. Mason jar niçoise salad

Ingredients

- 2 medium eggs

- 2 ½ cups halved green beans

- 3 (7-ounce) cans albacore tuna packed in water, drained and rinsed

- ¼ cup extra-virgin olive oil

- 2 tablespoons red wine vinegar

- 2 tablespoons diced red onion

- 2 tablespoons chopped fresh parsley leaves

- 1 tablespoon chopped fresh tarragon leaves

- 1 ½ teaspoons Dijon mustard

- Kosher salt and freshly ground black pepper, to taste

- 1 cup halved cherry tomatoes

- 4 cups torn butter lettuce

- 3 cups arugula leaves

- 12 Kalamata olives

- 1 lemon, cut into wedges (optional)

Directions

a) Place the eggs in a large saucepan and cover with cold water by 1 inch. Bring to a boil and cook for 1 minute. Cover the pot with a tight-fitting lid and remove from the heat; let sit for 8 to 10 minutes.

b) Meanwhile, in a large pot of boiling salted water, blanch the green beans until bright green in color, about 2 minutes. Drain and cool in a bowl of ice water. Drain well. Drain the eggs and let cool before peeling and cutting the eggs in half lengthwise.

c) In a large bowl, combine the tuna, olive oil, vinegar, onion, parsley, tarragon, and Dijon until just combined; season with salt and pepper to taste.

d) Divide the tuna mixture into 4 (32-ounce) wide-mouth glass jars with lids. Top with green beans, eggs, tomatoes, butter lettuce, arugula, and olives. Refrigerate for up to 3 days.

e) To serve, shake contents of a jar. Serve immediately, with lemon wedges if desired.

87.Spicy tuna bowls

Ingredients

- 1 cup long-grain brown rice
- 3 tablespoons olive oil mayonnaise
- 3 tablespoons Greek yogurt
- 1 tablespoon sriracha sauce, or more to taste
- 1 tablespoon lime juice
- 2 teaspoons reduced-sodium soy sauce
- 2 (5-ounce) cans albacore tuna, drained and rinsed
- Kosher salt and freshly ground black pepper, to taste
- 2 cups shredded kale
- 1 tablespoon toasted sesame seeds
- 2 teaspoons toasted sesame oil
- 1 ½ cups diced English cucumber
- ½ cup pickled ginger
- 3 green onions, thinly sliced
- ½ cup shredded roasted nori

Directions

a) Cook the rice according to package instructions in 2 cups water in a medium saucepan; set aside.

b) In a small bowl, whisk together the mayonnaise, yogurt, sriracha, lime juice, and soy sauce. Spoon 2 tablespoons of the mayonnaise mixture into a second bowl, cover, and refrigerate. Stir the tuna into the remaining mayo mixture and gently toss to combine; season with salt and pepper to taste.

c) In a medium bowl, combine the kale, sesame seeds, and sesame oil; season with salt and pepper to taste.

d) Divide the rice into meal prep containers. Top with tuna mixture, kale mixture, cucumber, ginger, green onions, and nori. Refrigerate for up to 3 days.

e) To serve, drizzle with the mayonnaise mixture.

88.Steak cobb salad

Balsamic vinaigrette

- 3 tablespoons extra-virgin olive oil
- 4 $\frac{1}{2}$ teaspoons balsamic vinegar
- 1 clove garlic, pressed
- 1 $\frac{1}{2}$ teaspoons dried parsley flakes
- $\frac{1}{4}$ teaspoon dried basil
- $\frac{1}{4}$ teaspoon dried oregano

Salad

- 4 medium eggs
- 1 tablespoon unsalted butter
- 12 ounces' steak
- 2 teaspoons olive oil
- Kosher salt and freshly ground black pepper, to taste
- 8 cups baby spinach
- 2 cups cherry tomatoes, halved
- $\frac{1}{2}$ cup pecan halves
- $\frac{1}{2}$ cup crumbled reduced-fat feta cheese

Directions

a) FOR THE BALSAMIC VINAIGRETTE: Whisk together the olive oil, balsamic vinegar, sugar, garlic, parsley, basil, oregano, and mustard (if using) in a medium bowl. Cover and refrigerate for up to 3 days.

b) Place the eggs in a large saucepan and cover with cold water by 1 inch. Bring to a boil and cook for 1 minute. Cover the pot with a tight-fitting lid and remove from heat; let sit for 8 to 10 minutes. Drain well and let cool before peeling and slicing.

c) Melt the butter in a large skillet over medium-high heat. Using paper towels, pat both sides of the steak dry. Drizzle with the olive oil and season with salt and pepper. Add the steak to the skillet and cook, flipping once, until cooked through to desired doneness, 3 to 4 minutes per side for medium-rare. Let rest 10 minutes before cutting into bite-size pieces.

d) To assemble the salads, place spinach into meal prep containers; top with arranged rows of steak, eggs, tomatoes, pecans, and feta. Cover and refrigerate for up to 3 days. Serve with the balsamic vinaigrette or desired dressing.

89.Sweet potato nourish bowls

Ingredients

- 2 medium sweet potatoes, peeled and cut into 1-inch chunks

- 3 tablespoons extra-virgin olive oil, divided

- $\frac{1}{2}$ teaspoon smoked paprika

- Kosher salt and freshly ground black pepper, to taste

- 1 cup farro

- 1 bunch lacinato kale, shredded

- 1 tablespoon freshly squeezed lemon juice

- 1 cup shredded red cabbage

- 1 cup halved cherry tomatoes

- $\frac{3}{4}$ cup Crispy Garbanzo Beans

- 2 avocados, halved, pitted, and peeled

Directions

a) Preheat the oven to 400 degrees F. Line a baking sheet with parchment paper.

b) Place the sweet potatoes on the prepared baking sheet. Add 1 ½ tablespoons of the olive oil and the paprika, season with salt and pepper, and gently toss to combine. Arrange in a single layer and bake for 20 to 25 minutes, turning once, until easily pierced with a fork.

c) Cook the farro according to package instructions; set aside.

d) Combine the kale, lemon juice, and the remaining 1 ½ tablespoons olive oil in a medium bowl. Massage the kale until well combined and season with salt and pepper to taste.

e) Divide farro into meal prep containers. Top with sweet potatoes, cabbage, tomatoes, and crispy garbanzos. Refrigerate for up to 3 days. Serve with the avocado.

90. Thai chicken buddha bowls

Ingredients

Spicy peanut sauce

- 3 tablespoons creamy peanut butter

- 2 tablespoons freshly squeezed lime juice

- 1 tablespoon reduced-sodium soy sauce

- 2 teaspoons dark brown sugar

- 2 teaspoons sambal oelek (ground fresh chile paste)

Salad

- 1 cup farro

- $\frac{1}{4}$ cup chicken stock

- 1 $\frac{1}{2}$ tablespoons sambal oelek (ground fresh chile paste)

- 1 tablespoon light brown sugar

- 1 tablespoon freshly squeezed lime juice

- 1 pound boneless, skinless chicken breasts, cut into 1-inch chunks

- 1 tablespoon cornstarch

- 1 tablespoon fish sauce

- 1 tablespoon olive oil

- 2 cloves garlic, minced

- 1 shallot, minced

- 1 tablespoon freshly grated ginger

- Kosher salt and freshly ground black pepper, to taste

- 2 cups shredded kale

- 1 $\frac{1}{2}$ cups shredded purple cabbage

- 1 cup bean sprouts

- 2 carrots, peeled and grated

- $\frac{1}{2}$ cup fresh cilantro leaves

- $\frac{1}{4}$ cup roasted peanuts

Directions

a) FOR THE PEANUT SAUCE: Whisk together the peanut butter, lime juice, soy sauce, brown sugar, sambal oelek, and 2 to 3 tablespoons water in a small bowl. Cover and refrigerate for up to 3 days.

b) Cook the farro according to package instructions; set aside.

c) While the farro cooks, in a small bowl, whisk together the stock, sambal oelek, brown sugar, and lime juice; set aside.

d) In a large bowl, combine the chicken, cornstarch, and fish sauce, toss to coat, and let the chicken absorb the cornstarch for a few minutes.

e) Heat the olive oil in a large skillet over medium heat. Add the chicken and cook until golden, 3 to 5 minutes. Add the garlic, shallot, and ginger and continue to cook, stirring frequently, until fragrant, about 2 minutes. Stir in the stock mixture and cook until slightly thickened, about 1 minute. Season with salt and pepper to taste.

f) Divide the farro into meal prep containers. Top with chicken, kale, cabbage, bean sprouts, carrots, cilantro, and peanuts. Will keep covered in the refrigerator 3 to 4 days. Serve with the spicy peanut sauce.

91.Thai peanut chicken wraps

Ingredients

Coconut curry peanut sauce

- $\frac{1}{4}$ cup light coconut milk
- 3 tablespoons creamy peanut butter
- 1 $\frac{1}{2}$ tablespoons seasoned rice wine vinegar
- 1 tablespoon reduced-sodium soy sauce
- 2 teaspoons dark brown sugar
- 1 teaspoon chili garlic sauce
- $\frac{1}{4}$ teaspoon yellow curry powder

Wrap

- 2 $\frac{1}{2}$ cups leftover diced rotisserie chicken
- 2 cups shredded Napa cabbage
- 1 cup thinly sliced red bell pepper
- 2 carrots, peeled and cut into matchsticks
- 1 $\frac{1}{2}$ tablespoons freshly squeezed lime juice
- 1 tablespoon olive oil mayonnaise
- Kosher salt and freshly ground black pepper, to taste

241

- 3 ounces reduced-fat cream cheese, at room temperature

- 1 teaspoon freshly grated ginger

- 4 (8-inch) sun-dried tomato tortilla wraps

Directions

a) FOR THE COCONUT CURRY PEANUT SAUCE: Whisk together the coconut milk, peanut butter, rice wine vinegar, soy sauce, brown sugar, chili garlic sauce, and curry powder in a small bowl. Set aside 3 tablespoons for the chicken; refrigerate the remainder until ready to serve.

b) In a large bowl, combine the chicken and the 3 tablespoons peanut sauce and toss until coated.

c) In a medium bowl, combine the cabbage, bell pepper, carrots, lime juice, and mayonnaise; season with salt and pepper to taste.

d) In a small bowl, combine the cream cheese and ginger; season with salt and pepper to taste.

e) Spread the cream cheese mixture evenly on the tortillas, leaving a 1-inch border. Top with the chicken and the cabbage mixture. Fold in sides by about 1 inch, then roll up tightly from the bottom. Will keep covered in the refrigerator 3 to 4 days. Serve each wrap with coconut curry peanut sauce.

92. Turkey spinach pinwheels

Ingredients

- 1 slice cheddar cheese
- 2 ounces thinly sliced turkey breast
- $\frac{1}{2}$ cup baby spinach
- 1 (8-inch) spinach tortilla
- 6 baby carrots
- $\frac{1}{4}$ cup grapes
- 5 cucumber slices

Directions

a) Place the cheese, turkey, and spinach in the center of the tortilla. Bring the bottom edge of the tortilla tightly over the spinach and fold in the sides. Roll up until the top of the tortilla is reached. Cut into 6 pinwheels.

b) Place pinwheels, carrots, grapes, and cucumber slices into a meal prep container. Keeps covered in the refrigerator for 2 to 3 days.

93. Turkey taco salad

Ingredients

- 1 tablespoon olive oil
- 1 ½ pounds ground turkey
- 1 (1.25-ounce) package taco seasoning
- 8 cups shredded romaine lettuce
- ½ cup pico de gallo (homemade or store-bought)
- ½ cup Greek yogurt
- ½ cup shredded Mexican cheese blend
- 1 lime, cut into wedges

Directions

a) Heat the olive oil in a large skillet over medium-high heat. Add the ground turkey and cook until browned, 3 to 5 minutes, making sure to crumble the meat as it cooks; stir in the taco seasoning. Drain excess fat.

b) Place the romaine lettuce in sandwich bags. Place the pico de gallo, yogurt, and cheese into separate 2-ounce Jell-O-shot cups with lids. Put it all—the turkey, romaine, pico de gallo, yogurt, cheese, and lime wedges—into meal prep containers.

94. Very green mason jar salad

Ingredients

- ¾ cup pearled barley

- 1 cup fresh basil leaves

- ¾ cup 2% Greek yogurt

- 2 green onions, chopped

- 1 ½ tablespoons freshly squeezed lime juice

- 1 clove garlic, peeled

- Kosher salt and freshly ground black pepper, to taste

- ½ English cucumber, coarsely chopped

- 1 pound (4 small) zucchini, spiralized

- 4 cups shredded kale

- 1 cup frozen green peas, thawed

- ½ cup crumbled reduced-fat feta cheese

- ½ cup pea shoots

- 1 lime, cut into wedges (optional)

Directions

a) Cook the barley according to package instructions; let cool completely and set aside.

b) To make the dressing, combine the basil, yogurt, green onions, lime juice, and garlic in the bowl of a food processor and season with salt and pepper. Pulse until smooth, about 30 seconds to 1 minute.

c) Divide the dressing into 4 (32-ounce) wide mouth glass jars with lids. Top with cucumber, zucchini noodles, barley, kale, peas, feta, and pea shoots. Refrigerate for up to 3 days.

d) To serve, shake the contents in a jar. Serve immediately, with lime wedges, if desired.

95.Zucchini spring roll bowls

Ingredients

- 3 tablespoons creamy peanut butter

- 2 tablespoons freshly squeezed lime juice

- 1 tablespoon reduced-sodium soy sauce

- 2 teaspoons dark brown sugar

- 2 teaspoons sambal oelek (ground fresh chile paste)

- 1-pound medium shrimp, peeled and deveined

- 4 medium zucchini, spiralized

- 2 large carrots, peeled and grated

- 2 cups shredded purple cabbage

- $\frac{1}{3}$ cup fresh cilantro leaves

- $\frac{1}{3}$ cup basil leaves

- $\frac{1}{4}$ cup mint leaves

- $\frac{1}{4}$ cup chopped roasted peanuts

Directions

a) FOR THE PEANUT SAUCE: Whisk together the peanut butter, lime juice, soy sauce, brown sugar, sambal oelek, and 2 to 3 tablespoons water in a small bowl. Refrigerate for up to 3 days, until ready to serve.

b) In a large pot of boiling salted water, cook the shrimp until pink, about 3 minutes. Drain and cool in a bowl of ice water. Drain well.

c) Divide zucchini into meal prep containers. Top with shrimp, carrots, cabbage, cilantro, basil, mint, and peanuts. Will keep covered in the refrigerator 3 to 4 days. Serve with the spicy peanut sauce.

FREEZER MEALS

96. Butternut squash fritters

Ingredients

- 4 cups shredded butternut squash
- ⅓ cup white whole wheat flour
- 2 cloves garlic, minced
- 2 large eggs, beaten
- ½ teaspoon dried thyme
- ¼ teaspoon dried sage
- Pinch of nutmeg
- Kosher salt and freshly ground black pepper, to taste
- 2 tablespoons olive oil
- ¼ cup Greek yogurt (optional)
- 2 tablespoons chopped fresh chives (optional)

Directions

a) In a large bowl, combine the squash, flour, garlic, eggs, thyme, sage, and nutmeg; season with salt and pepper.

b) Heat the olive oil in a large skillet over medium-high heat. In batches, scoop about 2 tablespoons of batter for each fritter, add to the pan, and flatten with a spatula. Cook until the undersides are nicely golden brown, about 2 minutes. Flip and cook on the other side, 1 to 2 minutes longer. Transfer to a paper towel-lined plate.

c) Serve immediately, with Greek yogurt and chives if desired.

d) TO FREEZE: Place the cooked fritters on a baking sheet in a single layer; cover tightly with plastic wrap, and freeze overnight. Transfer to freezer bags and store in the freezer for up to 3 months. When ready to serve, bake at 350 degrees F for about 10 to 15 minutes, until warmed, flipping halfway. Transfer to a paper towel-lined plate.

97.Carrot ginger soup

Ingredients

- 2 pounds' carrots, peeled and chopped
- 1 sweet potato, peeled and chopped
- 1 sweet onion, chopped
- 3 cloves garlic
- 1 ($\frac{3}{4}$-inch) piece fresh ginger, peeled and sliced
- 1 teaspoon smoked paprika
- 2 bay leaves
- 6 cups vegetable stock, plus more if needed
- Kosher salt and freshly ground black pepper, to taste
- $\frac{1}{3}$ cup fresh cilantro leaves
- $\frac{1}{4}$ cup fresh mint leaves
- 2 tablespoons freshly squeezed lime juice
- $\frac{1}{3}$ cup heavy cream
- $\frac{1}{4}$ teaspoon smoked paprika (optional)

Directions

a) Combine the carrots, sweet potato, onion, garlic, ginger, paprika, bay leaves, and stock in a large Dutch oven; season with salt and pepper.

b) Bring to a boil; reduce the heat and simmer until the carrots are tender, 25 to 30 minutes. Stir in the cilantro, mint, and lime juice. Discard the bay leaves.

c) Puree with an immersion blender to desired consistency. If the soup is too thick, add more stock as needed.

d) Stir in the cream and cook until heated through, about 2 minutes. Serve immediately, garnished with paprika if desired.

e) TO FREEZE: Omit the cream until ready to serve. Portion the cooled soup into ziplock freezer bags and lay the bags flat in a single layer in the freezer. To serve, add the cream and reheat over low heat, stirring occasionally, until heated through.

98.Cheesy chicken and broccoli rice casserole

Ingredients

- 1 (6-ounce) package long-grain and wild rice mix
- 3 tablespoons unsalted butter
- 3 cloves garlic, minced
- 1 onion, diced
- 2 cups cremini mushrooms, quartered
- 1 stalk celery, diced
- $\frac{1}{2}$ teaspoon dried thyme
- 1 tablespoon all-purpose flour
- $\frac{1}{4}$ cup dry white wine
- 1 $\frac{1}{4}$ cups chicken stock
- Kosher salt and freshly ground black pepper, to taste
- 3 cups broccoli florets
- $\frac{1}{2}$ cup sour cream
- 2 cups leftover shredded rotisserie chicken
- 1 cup shredded reduced-fat cheddar cheese, divided
- 2 tablespoons chopped fresh parsley leaves (optional)

Directions

a) Preheat the oven to 375 degrees F.

b) Cook the rice mix according to package instructions; set aside.

c) Melt the butter in a large ovenproof skillet over medium-high heat. Add the garlic, onion, mushrooms, and celery and cook, stirring occasionally, until tender, 3 to 4 minutes. Stir in the thyme and cook until fragrant, about 1 minute.

d) Whisk in the flour until lightly browned, about 1 minute. Gradually whisk in the wine and stock. Cook, whisking constantly, until slightly thickened, 2 to 3 minutes; season with salt and pepper to taste.

e) Stir in the broccoli, sour cream, chicken, $\frac{1}{2}$ cup of the cheese, and the rice. If freezing the casserole for later use, stop here and skip to step 7. Otherwise, sprinkle with the remaining $\frac{1}{2}$ cup cheese.

f) Transfer the skillet to the oven and bake until the casserole is bubbly and heated through, 20 to 22 minutes. Serve immediately, garnished with parsley if desired.

g) Freeze.

99.Chicken and quinoa tortilla soup

Ingredients

Baked tortilla strips

- 4 corn tortillas, cut into thin strips
- ½ teaspoon chili powder, or more to taste
- Kosher salt and freshly ground black pepper, to taste
- 1 tablespoon olive oil

Soup

- 1 pound boneless, skinless chicken breasts
- Kosher salt and freshly ground black pepper, to taste
- 3 cloves garlic, minced
- 1 onion, diced
- 1 green bell pepper, diced
- 2 tablespoons tomato paste
- 1 tablespoon chili powder
- 1 ½ teaspoons ground cumin
- 1 teaspoon dried oregano
- 8 cups chicken stock

- 1 (28-ounce) can diced tomatoes

- 1 (15-ounce) can black beans, drained and rinsed

- 1 $\frac{1}{2}$ cups corn kernels (frozen, canned, or roasted)

- $\frac{1}{2}$ cup quinoa

- Juice of 1 lime

- $\frac{1}{2}$ cup chopped fresh cilantro leaves

- Optional garnishes: shredded cheddar cheese, minced red onion, jalapeño slices, cilantro leaves

Directions

a) FOR THE TORTILLA STRIPS: Preheat the oven to 375 degrees F. Lightly oil a baking sheet or coat with nonstick spray.

b) Spread the tortilla strips in a single layer on the prepared baking sheet; season with the chili powder, salt, and pepper and coat with nonstick spray. Bake until crisp and golden, 10 to 12 minutes, stirring halfway; set aside and let cool.

c) Heat the olive oil in a large stockpot or Dutch oven over medium heat. Season the chicken with salt and pepper. Add the chicken to the pot and cook until golden, 2 to 3 minutes per side; transfer to a plate and set aside.

d) Add the garlic, onion, and bell pepper to the pot and cook, stirring occasionally, until tender, 3 to 4 minutes. Stir in the tomato paste, chili powder, cumin, and oregano and cook until fragrant, about 1 minute. Stir in the chicken, along with the stock, tomatoes, black beans, and corn. Bring to a boil; reduce the heat and simmer, uncovered, until the chicken is tender and cooked through, 20 to 25 minutes. Remove the chicken from the pot and shred, using two forks.

e) Return the shredded chicken to the pot along with the quinoa and simmer, uncovered, until the quinoa is tender, 15 to 20 minutes. Stir in the lime juice and cilantro and season with salt and pepper to taste.

f) Serve immediately with the baked tortilla strips, and additional garnishes if desired.

100.   Turkey tamale pies with cornbread crust

Ingredients

Filling

- 1 tablespoon olive oil
- 1-pound ground turkey breast
- 2 cloves garlic, minced
- 1 onion, diced
- 1 medium poblano pepper, seeded and diced
- 2 teaspoons chili powder
- 1 teaspoon dried oregano
- $\frac{3}{4}$ teaspoon ground cumin
- Kosher salt and freshly ground black pepper, to taste
- 2 (14.5-ounce) cans Mexican-style stewed tomatoes
- 1 cup corn kernels
- 2 tablespoons chopped fresh cilantro leaves

Cheddar-cilantro cornbread crust

- $\frac{1}{2}$ cup yellow cornmeal
- $\frac{1}{4}$ cup all-purpose flour

- 1 teaspoon baking powder

- $\frac{1}{4}$ teaspoon kosher salt

- $\frac{3}{4}$ cup low-fat buttermilk

- 1 large egg

- 1 tablespoon unsalted butter, melted

- $\frac{3}{4}$ cup shredded extra-sharp cheddar cheese

- $\frac{1}{4}$ cup chopped fresh cilantro leaves

Directions

a) Preheat the oven to 425 degrees F. Lightly oil 6 (10-ounce) ramekins or coat with nonstick spray.

b) FOR THE FILLING: Heat the olive oil in a large skillet over medium-high heat. Add the ground turkey, garlic, onion, and poblano. Cook until the turkey has browned, 3 to 5 minutes, making sure to crumble the turkey as it cooks. Stir in the chili powder, oregano, and cumin; season with salt and pepper. Drain excess fat.

c) Stir in the tomatoes and break them up with the back of a spoon. Bring to a simmer and stir in the corn and cilantro. Divide the mixture into the prepared ramekins.

d) FOR THE CRUST: Combine the cornmeal, flour, baking powder, and salt in a medium bowl. In a large glass measuring cup or another bowl, whisk together the buttermilk, egg, and butter. Pour the wet mixture over the dry Ingredients and stir, using a rubber spatula, just until moist. Add the cheese and cilantro, and gently toss to combine.

e) Top the filling in the ramekins with the crust mixture in an even layer. Place on a baking sheet and bake until golden brown and the crust is set, about 25 minutes. Let cool 10 minutes before serving, garnished with additional cilantro leaves.

f) TO FREEZE: Don't make the crust until the day of serving. Prepare the filling to the end of step 3, then cover the individual ramekins tightly with plastic wrap. Freeze for up to 3 months. To serve, remove the plastic wrap. Cover the ramekins with aluminum foil and bake at 425 degrees F for 45 minutes while you make the crust. Uncover the ramekins and top with the crust mixture. Bake for an additional 20 to 30 minutes, until completely cooked through.

CONCLUSION

Eating right isn't just about saying no to the unhealthy stuff—it is about saying yes to the just-as-delicious alternative that are already prepped and waiting for you.